Contents

THE ONLINE SEARCHER'S COMPANION

William H Forrester
Jane L Rowlands

LIBRARY ASSOCIATION PUBLISHING
LONDON

© William H Forrester and Jane L Rowlands 2000

Published by
Library Association Publishing
7 Ridgmount Street
London WC1E 7AE

Library Association Publishing is wholly owned by The Library Association.

First published 2000

British Library Cataloguing in Publication Data
A catalogue record for this book is available from the British Library.

ISBN 1-85604-293-6

Typeset by the authors.

Printed and made in Great Britain by MPG Books Ltd, Bodmin, Cornwall.

Appendix 1 History of computers, online searching, and the Internet   111

Appendix 2 Modems   125

Appendix 3 Books and journals on online/Internet searching   137

Appendix 4 Major online database host services   145

Index   151

Introduction

Welcome to the first edition of *The online searcher's companion*. This book aims to explain, in as simple a manner as possible, what online searching is all about. We shall be covering all aspects of online searching from the pre-search stage, ie obtaining information from the person requesting an online search, to basic and advanced online searching, and to effectively searching the Internet.

But what do we mean by the term 'online searching'? Before the advent of CD-ROMs, online searching meant that you connected to a remote computer via a modem to perform some type of literature search. The modem was usually connected to a dumb terminal or a personal computer (PC).

With CD-ROMs, and the growth of public access catalogues (OPACs), online searching has come to mean the searching of any computerized database, no matter whether it's situated on your own PC's hard disk, on a CD-ROM, or on a remote database server, or, since most PCs nowadays can link to the Internet, to various world wide web sites.

The time for performing 'hand searches' through the printed versions of publications such as Index Medicus, Physics Abstracts, and so on, has long since passed. An online search is far quicker, as it can link multiple terms together and present the answer after a relatively short span of time.

This book is meant to be an aid to searching what we would call the traditional online sources. It therefore concentrates on searching online host systems, such as Data-Star, DIALOG, and FT Profile, and briefly explaining the resources on the web that can be used to retrieve relevant information and websites.

We have excluded mention of how to search CD-ROMs and OPACs simply because they usually have their own search software, either on the CD-ROM or as part of the library management system running the library's catalogue system. However, the ideas of Boolean logic and creating a search strategy are still of use, since they apply to whatever system you are searching.

This book is aimed at the novice online searcher, or at end-users who simply want to search the literature for themselves. It will also be useful for those people who are returning to searching after an absence. *The online searcher's companion* is a book that can be kept with you when searching, as a checklist of how to get the best out of your search.

Chapter 1 covers the pre-search stage, discussing what information is needed from the enquirer and what resources are required to plan and execute an online search.

Chapter 2 introduces the reader to the basic principles of searching, and explains how Boolean logic, the mainstay of online searching, works. It also describes the use of the adjacency and truncation operators.

Chapter 3 introduces the reader to more advanced methods of retrieving information and describes the use of descriptors (subject headings) and subheadings, field qualifiers, and how to limit a search to particular aspects of documents.

Chapter 4 concentrates solely on searching full-text databases and goes through techniques that are useful when searching these. Examples are taken mainly from FT Profile because it is one of the major sources in the UK full-text database field.

Chapter 5 mentions briefly that most of the major online hosts also have web page access, and gives examples of one or two. A fuller list is to be found in Appendix 4. The rest of Chapter 5 is devoted to the use of Internet search engines in retrieving relevant information.

Chapter 6 contrasts and compares the question of recall versus precision (or quantity versus quality), to see how both can be improved without sacrificing either. A list of ideas to improve both is discussed.

Chapter 7 contains five worked examples drawn from a variety of subjects. We go through the stages of analysing the topic, choosing search terms, and performing the search. The online hosts Data-Star and DIALOG are used.

There are four appendices at the end of the book. Appendix 1 covers the history of computing, online searching, and the Internet. Appendix 2 covers how a modem works, for those interested. Appendix 3 lists books and journals on the topics of online searching and the Internet. Appendix 4 lists information on all of the major online hosts, giving addresses, telephone numbers, contact details, and web page addresses where possible.

Chapter 1
The pre-search process

Introduction

So you want to carry out an online search. You're either doing the search for yourself or for a colleague or for a client. Are you familiar with the subject field in which you'll be searching? Have you identified the key terms? Have you decided which database(s) to use? These and other questions will be considered in this chapter.

What sort of information will be found?

There are thousands and thousands of different topics for which you may wish to search. But most queries tend to fall into two broad categories: basic searches for facts and figures, or descriptive text, and much more complex searches.

Basic searches

Basic searches cover the fairly simple enquiries where the user is looking for a particular fact, a particular set of figures, or a definition or description of a subject. Answers to most of these types of searches were traditionally found duplicated in different textbooks, encyclopaedias, and so on. Nowadays the Internet and the web, in particular, seem to be the first port of call.

Simply by loading your Web browser and using one of the Web search engines, eg AltaVista, you can search for anything you desire and find more than you want. In Chapter 5 we will be talking about how to use these Web search engines to find relevant information.

Traditional online services can also be used. Many of the full-text sources will have the information available either in a preformatted version or held in the body of the documents. Examples of these are company reports from various full-text databases, such as Dun & Bradstreet on DIALOG or full-text newspaper articles in the FT Profile databases.

More complex searches

These tend to be searches where there are no definitive facts that you can pull from a textbook, but are usually searches at the forefront of research. You usually find that you need to use several different sources to find the 'answers'. You may well be searching subjects that you are not familiar with.

The search may necessitate your having to assess, compare, and integrate the information retrieved and present it to your client as a complete report, eg market sector research reports or complex medical research, where there are differing results and outcomes. Even having done an online search, you may also need to contact outside agencies.

After reading this book, you should feel capable of handling both types of searches. But how do you start? Well, we would suggest first of all that you consider what needs to be done before you actually perform an online search.

The pre-search stage

Have all the necessary aids

If you are required to perform a search in a subject area unfamiliar to yourself, you will need to acquaint yourself with the topic. This can be done in various ways, but there are aids that you can use. These include the following.

Guides to the literature

These are usually books that take you through a particular subject, describing all the different forms of literature that you may find on the topic.

These may range through primary sources, such as research reports or journal articles, to secondary sources, such as textbooks on the topic, to tertiary sources, such as dictionaries and encyclopaedias.

Dictionaries, glossaries, encyclopaedias

With an unfamiliar subject, it is useful to make sure what the terms you have been given actually mean. There is a world of difference between arteriosclerosis and atherosclerosis, but it may not be clear that they are different until you have checked the dictionary definition.

Once you have an idea of what the topic is about, you can then read around it to get some basic ideas about the topic. This is vital because quite often the client you are doing the search for is unable to be present when you perform the actual search, and it will be your job to decide if you have found relevant references.

Even if you are doing the search for yourself, you still need to know something about the topic.

Database producers' manuals and newsletters

These are very useful, because they inform you as to how a particular database has been put together, what it does and doesn't contain, what the structure is, and quite often give examples of searches.

The newsletters are used to update the manuals and to inform you about changes to the database.

Thesauri and classification schemes

These are required if you wish to perform your search correctly and exhaustively. Many databases are indexed using set subjects arranged in a thesaurus or a classification scheme and not by words given in the titles and abstracts of items.

Many of these thesauri and/or classification schemes are hierarchically structured. This means that they go from broad terms to narrower, more specific, terms. Using a thesaurus, you can find out if there are any more specific terms, or even related terms, available for the topic for which you are searching.

Using these thesauri and so on the indexers working on a particular journal will usually use the most specific term possible when assigning index terms (subject headings) to an item. For example, if the indexers have a paper on eye cataracts, they will index it specifically under cataract and not under eye diseases.

Figure 1.1 shows an extract from the MeSH (medical subject headings) thesaurus showing the cataract entry.

Cataract
   C11.510.245
   lens opacity; do not confuse X ref PSEUDOAPHAKIA (a synonym for membranous cataract) with PSEUDOPHAKIA, the presence of an intraocular lens after cataract extraction
   X   Cataract, Membranous
   X   Lens Opacities
   X   Pseudoaphakia
   Cataract/surgery see Cataract Extraction

Cataract Extraction
   E4.540.208+
   do not use /util except by MeSH definition
   ENZYMATIC ZONULOLYSIS was heading 1963-96
   see related
         Aphakia, Postcataract
         Lenses, Intraocular
         Pseudophakia
   X   Enzymatic Zonulolysis

Cataract, Membranous see Cataract
   C11.510.245

Catarrhina see Cercopithecidae
   B2.649.801.400.130+

Castastomus see Cypriniformes
   B2.493.200+

Catastrophic Health Insurance see Insurance, Major Medical
   N3.219.521.576.343.533

Figure 1.1 *MeSH Thesaurus*

Online service manuals and newsletters

Since you will be searching online hosts, it is important that you have their system manuals to hand. The system manuals will tell you what commands to use in order to search for, print, or save items, how to limit a search, and so on.

They will usually have individual sheets about each database hosted, giving a breakdown of the structure of each record, what field names are used, and what limits you can apply.

Figures 1.2 and 1.3 show the front and back from a typical DIALOG blue sheet.

238

CURRENT TECHNOLOGY DATABASE

FILE DESCRIPTION

Current Technology Database is an abstracting and indexing service covering approximately 350 journals from the U.K. and the U.S. in technology, engineering, and allied subject areas. The file corresponds to the printed products *Current Technology Index* and *Catchword and Trade Name Index*. Abstracts are available from January 1993 to the present.

SUBJECT COVERAGE

Current Technology Database covers all areas of technology and engineering, plus allied areas of science and management. The following are the main subjects covered:

- Aerospace
- Chemical Technology and Engineering
- Communications Engineering
- Computers and Control
- Construction
- Design
- Electrical and Electronic Engineering
- Energy
- Ergonomics
- Food, Farming, Fishing, and Forestry
- Health and Safety
- Management Services
- Mechanical and Production Engineering
- Medical Technology
- Metallurgy
- Military Technology
- Mineral Extraction and Processing
- Photography and Cinematography
- Pollution, Waste and Water Engineering
- Printing, Paper, and Packaging
- Quality Assurance, Training and Standards
- Radio and Television
- Road, Rail, and Sea Transport
- Science and Measurement
- Sound and Video Recording
- Textiles, Leather and Wood

TIPS

USE FILE 238
for all areas of technology and engineering, especially for British-oriented searches.

USE BRITISH SPELLING
in addition to American spelling for comprehensive retrieval.
SELECT (ALUMINUM OR ALUMINIUM)/TI,DE

USE RANK
to find experts working in an area of interest.
**SELECT THIN(W)FILMS AND PHOTOVOLTAGE;
RANK AU**

DIALOG FILE DATA

Inclusive Dates: 1981 to the present;
Abstracts from January 1993 to the present
Update Frequency: Monthly
File Size: Approximately 240,000 records as of March 1997

CONTACT

Current Technology Database is provided by Bowker Saur, a part of Reed Business Information Ltd. Questions concerning file content should be directed to:

Peter Ellway, Editor, Current Technology Index
Bowker Saur
Maypole House, Maypole Road
East Grinstead, West Sussex, RH19 1HU
United Kingdom
Telephone: 44 (0)1342 330165
Fax: 44 (0)1342 330197
E-Mail: pellway@bowker-saur.co.uk

Figure 1.2 *Blue sheet from DIALOG*

```
FILE 238                    CURRENT TECHNOLOGY DATABASE


SAMPLE RECORD

              DIALOG(R)File 238:Current Technology Database
              (c) 1997 The Reed Publishing Company. All rts. reserv.

      AA=     0091021   CTI NUMBER: 9604782
      /TI     Anomalous photovoltage in Cd0.25Zn0.75Te thin films
      AU=     AUTHOR(S): Samanta, B.;  Chaudhuri, A. K.;  Sharma, S. L.
 JN=, SO=     JOURNAL: Journal of Physics D. Applied Physics
      SO=     SOURCE: 29 (1) 14 Jan 96 p.188-94.  il.refs.
      PY=     PUBLICATION YEAR: 1996
      SN=     ISSN: 0022-3727
              BLDSC SHELF MARK: 5036.240
      LA=     LANGUAGE: English

      /AB     ABSTRACT:  This anomalous photovoltage is described as a combined effect of
              mainly p-p+ junctions at the grain boundaries and surface band bending. A
              new method has been developed to enhance the photovoltage by placing a fine
              mesh in front of the substrate during film deposition. The enhancement is
              explained with the help of a trap-induced space charge model.   (Abstract
              uses original text)

      /DE     DESCRIPTORS: Films;   Vacuum deposited cadmium zinc telluride;   Anomalous
              photovoltage
```

Figure 1.3 *Blue sheet from DIALOG (reverse)*

Obtain information about the enquiry

Before you can perform any search you need to find out what is required, ie the subject matter, how comprehensive a search is to be, any limitations, and so on.

All this information can be obtained by questioning the person who requested the search and by using the above aids.

What information do you need to obtain from the enquirer?

Ask the enquirer to provide

• a brief written, or oral summary of the search topic,

- a list of words or phrases likely to appear in relevant documents,

- some recent relevant references on the topic, so that you can read them and understand what the enquirer wants.

Try to establish

- how comprehensive a search is required. Find out from the enquirer what depth of information is required, eg simple, straightforward information; very complex information; anything in between.

- how many references the enquirer expects you to find. This can give a measure of how rare or how common the subject is. You may need to question further in order to narrow down the specific topic if the subject field is too large.

- if there are any limitations. This may cover the date range (how far back to search); any language restrictions (pointless to find items that are in a language the enquirer can't read); type of material (the enquirer may require only one type of material, eg journal articles rather than books). Other limits may include: human/animal; place of publication; age ranges, eg children; and so on.

- how urgent the search is — how soon does the enquirer need the results. The date by which a search is required may affect how the search is performed and how many results are found. If results are needed urgently, a quick and 'dirty' search may well produce relevant items, but a less urgent search will usually find more relevant items because of the time to consider all the factors.

Most search services offered by libraries or other agencies usually have a search request form that either staff or the enquirer can complete.

Figure 1.4 shows one that the BMA Library currently uses.

BMA LIBRARY BMA

BMA House, Tavistock Square, London, WC1H 9JP. Tel: 0171-383 6630

LITERATURE SEARCH REQUEST FORM

Name:	Mem No:	Date:

Address:

Telephone No:	Fax No:

TYPE OF SEARCH:	Please Tick:
Quick Search: {Up to 10 references from a well-documented subject, free of charge.}	
Online Search: {See reverse for details.}	

LANGUAGE(S) REQUIRED:	RANGE OF YEARS TO SEARCH: {Online search only.}
English:	Last 3 years:
French:	Last 5 years:
German:	Last 10 years:
Spanish:	As far back as possible:
Other:	Your choice:

DESCRIPTION OF SUBJECT: {General description of what is required.}

RELEVANT KEYWORDS:

DATABASE TO SEARCH: {See overleaf for a brief description of some additional databases available.}
MEDLINE:
Excerpta Medica:
Psychological Abstracts:
Biosis:
Other:

Figure 1.4 *Literature search request form*

How do you obtain the information from the enquirer?

This is normally carried out by what is known as the pre-search interview, and it is very important that it is approached with the right attitude.

Often online searches requested by clients are not carried out in the client's presence. Therefore, the information gathered from the interview is vital if you are to ensure that relevant items are found during the online search process.

Getting clients to tell you exactly what they want you to search for can be an art in itself. But it is a necessary process, because you will be assigning search terms and constructing strategies based on what the client has told you.

If you get it wrong, it can be very expensive (you may well have to repeat the search free of charge).

So what can you do to bring out the correct information?

- Use a search request form as an aide-mémoire. Having this in front of you when speaking to the client is a very simple way of remembering what you need to ask.

- Try to establish a rapport with the client.

  — An online searcher needs to be skilled in person-to-person communication and needs to make a good impression.

  — Most searchers usually have knowledge of the subject field in which they search. Most of their clients work in the same subject field.

— Try to put the client at ease by being able to discuss the topic competently, and try to show that you will do your best.

- Discuss the general subject area of the query. You don't need to be an expert in the client's specialist area, but you should be able to discuss the general subject area of the search in some detail. This should allow you, the searcher, to design an efficient online search strategy and allow you to know whether the search results you find are relevant.

- Try to ask open-ended questions. Always try to ask questions in such a way that the client can't answer them with a simple yes or no. This should enable you to draw out of the client lots of useful information. Unfortunately, it can also lead to their life story!

Analyse the search topics

Analysing the search topic is the most vital part of an online search. If this is done incorrectly, then you won't find what you are looking for. Having analysed the search topic you then need to break it down into its component terms.

This will involve:

- Separating the 'wheat from the chaff', ie filtering out the irrelevant and unnecessary words from the search statement.

- Using any of the aids mentioned above, especially thesauri, to decide on the correct terms to use and any synonyms of those terms.

- Checking back with the enquirer, if possible, to make sure that your analysis of the search topic is correct.

How do you analyse a search topic?

At the end of the pre-search interview, you will have obtained from the enquirer a statement of what the search topic is about, for example:

1 Please find papers on the link between aluminium and Alzheimer's disease.

2 I'm looking for items that talk about the use of aspirin in helping to reduce the risk of heart attacks.

3 Are there any links between detergents and cancer?

Before you even consider going online, you need to split the statement up into relevant terms and decide which are separate concepts, which are synonyms, and which terms are irrelevant to the search.

Taking (1) from above, the only relevant, specific terms are:

aluminium and Alzheimer's disease

The others are all irrelevant to the actual search. 'Papers' indicates that the enquirer needs journal articles, whilst 'link between' means find the two terms in the same papers.

But we also need to think about synonyms and alternative spelling of the terms.

Using some of the aids listed above, eg dictionaries and thesauri, we then obtain:

Concept 1   aluminium
                      aluminum (note American spelling)
                      Al (the chemical symbol)

Concept 2   Alzheimer's disease
                      senile dementia

Similarly with (2) above, the relevant terms are:

aspirin and heart attacks

'Risk' isn't really relevant unless the search produces hundreds of references and you need another term to reduce the number to a manageable level.

Again, using the aids above, we then obtain the following concepts:

Concept 1   aspirin
                      acetylsalicylic acid

Concept 2   heart attack
                      myocardial infarction

So you now know what terms are needed to perform the search. Before carrying out a search, you need to decide which database(s) to use.

Decide on the database

Many factors can dictate which database is used to perform the online search. These include the following.

Subject coverage

- Does the database cover the topic you are interested in? To find out, consult the database guides, the online hosts' manuals, and perhaps go online and perform a 'quick and dirty' search across many similar databases.

- By a 'quick and dirty' search, we mean one where you simply enter the most obvious search term(s) and see how many 'hits' occur in each of the selected databases.

- Data-Star, and many other hosts, will allow you to run a search over pre-selected database groups as well as allowing you to choose specific ones. The results of such a search will usually inform you which database(s) would be most useful to search. Figure 1.5 gives an example of a cross-database search.

Indexing

Do you know how the items in the database are indexed? Is it done consistently? Are changes applied retrospectively?

In other words, do you have to use different search terms to search the same concept over different time spans? If so, how long is it going to take to type all the terms in?

Does the database have a good thesaurus available? Is it readily accessible by you? If so, use it!

Up-to-dateness

You need to check how often the database is updated. Your enquirer may want very up-to-date information. Searching a database that is six months behind the current literature may not be as useful as searching one that is only one month behind.

Date range

How far back does the database go? If you are trying to perform a comprehensive search of the literature, you need a database

```
D--S -- SEARCH MODE -- ENTER SEARCH TERMS

CROS     1_:  minoxidil and baldness

ACQS        AIDSLINE NLM 1980 -- SEP'99              0   OF      184504
AEZT    F   AERZTEZEITUNG '84--WK32/'99              0   OF      280526
AMED        ALLIED & ALTERNATIVE MEDICINE'85--       0   OF      110866
BIAF        BIOSIS UEF AUTHORITY FILE                0   OF        1799
BIOL        BIOSIS PREVIEWS 1993 TO DATE            10   OF     3669946
BIYY        BIOSIS PREVIEWS 1970 TO 1992            61   OF     8125957
CANC        CANCERLIT NLM '86 -- NOV '98             4   OF     1024224
CAZZ        CANCERLIT NLM '63 -- NOV '98             4   OF     1441614
CBIB        C.CONTENTS: BIBLIOGRAPHIC, 1995--       20   OF     4658387
CTOC    F   C.CONTENTS: CONTENTS TABLES,1995--       1   OF      254918
DPMS    F   PHARMA MARKETING SERVICE '87--           0   OF       39599
ELBI        ELSEVIER BIOBASE -- 1994 TO 99/34        2   OF     1218337
EMBA        EMBASE ALERT LATEST 8 WEEKS              1   OF       71206
EMYY        EMBASE 1993 TO DATE                     16   OF     2591939
EMZZ        EMBASE 1974 TO DATE                     75   OF     7726628
ERDB    F   EUR. RES. & DEVT DATABASE                0   OF       84542
ETHI    F   BIOETHICSLINE 1973 -- 9908               0   OF       60923
EVNT        EVENTLINE                                0   OF      241619
GPGP    F   GENERAL PRACTITIONER '87--              32   OF       74565
HLPA        HEALTHSTAR 1990 -- SEP 1999              0   OF     1774268
HLTH        HEALTH '76 -- TO DATE                  203   OF      682368
HLZZ        HEALTHSTAR 1975 -- SEP 1999             35   OF     3449753
HSLI        HSELINE: HEALTH & SAFETY '77--           0   OF      196535
HUMN        CAB HEALTH '73 -- 07/1999                0   OF      668871
IAPV        INCIDENCE & PREVALENCE (IPD) '88--       0   OF       15723
IOWA        IDIS DRUG FILE '66--                    15   OF      513125
IPMR        IMSWORLD R&D FOCUS MEETINGS DIARY        0   OF         570
JIST        JICST--EPLUS:JAPANESE SCI/TECH 85--      2   OF     3256921
LANC    F   LANC: 1986 TO DATE                      10   OF       47668
MANT        MANTIS 1997 -- JULY 1999                 2   OF       42246
MCNF        MEDICONF: MEDICAL CONF & EVENTS          0   OF       61680
MEYY        MEDLINE 1993--OCT.'99 (--ED990819)      12   OF     2592321
MEZZ        MEDLINE 1966--OCT.'99 (--ED990819)      62   OF    10065936
NAHL        CINAHL (R) '82--                        20   OF      481621
NEJM    F   NEW ENGLAND JOURNAL OF MED. 85--         1   OF       18566
NSCI    F   NEW SCIENTIST 1994--                     0   OF       23241
PASC        PASC: 1984 TO WEEK34 '99                19   OF     7859253
PSYC        PSYCINFO, 1887 TO SEPTEMBER '99          0   OF     1597755
SCIN        SCIENCE CIT. INDEX '87-- WK34/'99      107   OF     9996088
SC86        SCIENCE CITATION INDEX: '80--'86        10   OF     4495788
SERL        SERLINE:BIOMED. JOURNALS DEC.1998        0   OF       89501
```

Figure 1.5 *Cross-database search on Data-Star for the terms Minoxidil and Baldness*

that goes back a good number of years, not just one or two.

Journal range

How many journals are indexed by the database? Are the core journals that cover the topic indexed in the database you wish to use? If so, are they cover-to-cover or just selected items? If correspondence is of interest, then you require the former.

Are the journals likely to be available locally? How easy would it be to supply photocopies of items retrieved? Obtaining them via interlibrary loan could be time-consuming and expensive.

Please note that many of the databases found on online hosts tend to be bibliographic in nature rather than full-text, ie they contain references to where the full-text is to be found. Hence the need to obtain photocopies, as above.

Language

Is the database you wish to use in English or is it predominantly in another language? Can your enquirer handle languages other than English?

Fields and limiting

Are the relevant fields you wish to search available in the records of the items in the database? Can you search specific fields and can you limit to certain categories, eg English language items, particular date ranges, human and/or animal.

Cost

Is the database you wish to search too costly? Some of the full text databases can be very expensive to search. Is cost a factor?

All of the above factors ask questions of the searcher. Where can you find the answers? Simply by consulting the database producers' and the online hosts' service manuals and newsletters, as mentioned earlier in this chapter. They will give you all the information you need to decide which database to search.

Decide on the host

You now know what to search for and in which database(s), but which online host should you use?

You may have access to several different hosts, all of which will have a core of similar databases, but they will each have some unique ones.

Database hosts exist so that database producers don't have to go to the expense of setting up their own online host system. With thousands of databases available, it would make life very complicated for online searchers if they had to connect to a different system each time they wanted to search another database.

Usually the database producer licenses a particular host, or several hosts, to hold its information and pay the database producer royalties for each record looked at or downloaded. This cost is then passed on to the online searcher as charges for accessing particular databases. Charges will vary depending on what sort of a return the database producer and host system want to get on their investment.

Therefore, several hosts may carry the same database simply because they are trying to compete with other hosts for the online searcher's money, or because they want to offer a suite of databases all in the same subject area, eg Data-Star is particularly strong in medicine and health care.

Factors that can help in deciding which database to use include:

Cost

Is the database cheaper from one of the hosts you have access to? If so, use that host.

Time

How much time have you got to do the search? If the information is needed urgently, then you may have to make some quick decisions as to which database to search. If there is a choice between two or three then you may simply choose the one with which you are most familiar.

Will the enquirer be with you? If so, the search is likely to take longer because you will need to talk to him or her during the search and ask if what you are finding is what is wanted.

This can usually lead on to completely different topics, as the search may throw up other terms that the enquirer will want you to pursue.

Command language

A command language is unique to each host system and is the software the host uses to interrogate, and possibly reformat, the information contained within the databases it hosts.

Are you very familiar with the command language of one host compared to another? DIALOG and Data-Star have similar databases, but use completely different command syntax to perform searches.

Choosing the one you are most familiar with can hasten the search process and so reduce time online.

Database structure

Has the database been mounted differently on different hosts? Can you search more fields using one host than another? Do they have different limits? Are the subject headings handled differently? What sort of truncation can you use?

Is the database split into several segments or does it exist as one large database?

Communications

Is one host cheaper to access than another via the telecommunications services? Can you connect to one host at a faster speed than another.

Searching across more than one database

Will the host allow you to use the same search strategy over more than one database? In medicine, searching the MEDLINE, Embase, and Biosis database virtually ensures total coverage of the medical literature. It is possible on Data-Star to search all three and remove any duplicates found.

Summary

In this chapter, we have introduced you to the pre-search stage of an online search, and suggested what type of information is to be found. We have talked about the search aids that you may use to help you make decisions on what subject to search for and which database to search, ie guides to the literature; dictionaries and encyclopaedias; database producers' manuals and newsletters; thesauri and classification schemes; and online host service manuals and newsletters.

We hope also to have informed you what information is required from the enquirer and how to go about obtaining it. We have also shown you how to analyse the search topic into its component concepts and how to decide on what database and host to use when performing the actual online search.

The next chapter will describe the basic search techniques that anyone performing any sort of search needs to know.

Chapter 2
Basic search techniques

Introduction

This chapter will explain the basic techniques used in performing online searches. The use of Boolean logic, i.e. the use of the operators AND, OR, and NOT will be shown by examples as well as by the use of Venn diagrams. We shall then go on to talk about the use of truncation and adjacency operators, all of which will be explained using examples of actual usage.

But first let us reprise Chapter 1 and look at a typical search request.

Search request

Let us look at an example of a search request and how this can be used to demonstrate the use of the Boolean operators.

Search request:

> I'm looking for items that talk about the use of aspirin in helping to reduce the risk of heart attacks.

Using the techniques discussed in Chapter 1, this search request could be analysed to give the search terms:

aspirin
acetylsalicylic acid
heart attack
myocardial infarction

After analysing the search, the next process is to consider which of the search terms are separate concepts and which are synonyms.

Looking at the list above, we can split it into two separate concepts:

Concept 1:   aspirin
acetylsalicylic acid

Concept 2:   heart attack
myocardial infarction

So acetylsalicylic acid is another name (a synonym) for aspirin and myocardial infarction is the MeSH term for heart attack.

These concepts and synonyms are now ready to be combined.

Boolean operators

The operators AND, OR, and NOT are known as Boolean operators, after the English mathematician George Boole (1815-1864). These operators are used to combine search terms in order to produce relevant results: they are vital for effective online searching. We will use Venn diagrams to explain how they work.

In Figures 2.1 to 2.3 cats and dogs are both represented by circles. Each circle represents the literature that exists on dogs and on cats. The rectangle represents the literature of all subjects.

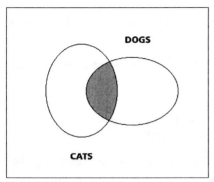

Figure 2.1 *Use of AND*

1 Cats AND dogs: the intersection of the two circles represents a search on two concepts linking them using the Boolean operator AND. The search will retrieve only items that contain both cats AND dogs.

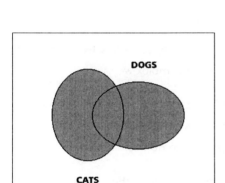

Figure 2.2 *Use of OR*

2 Cats OR dogs: the Boolean operator OR is very useful when linking like concepts (synonyms) together. In this example we want to retrieve anything and everything that mentions cats or dogs. Since each of the circles represents the total literature on both topics, then we will retrieve every single item that mentions cats and/or dogs.

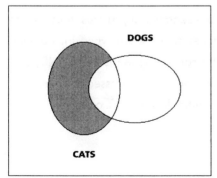

Figure 2.3 *Use of NOT*

3 Cats NOT dogs: the Boolean operator NOT can be very useful in restricting or limiting searches to specific subjects. In our example we want to find every item on cats, but don't want any that mention dogs as well. The NOT operator does this by excluding any items that have the term dogs anywhere in them.

Getting back to our search example above, in order to combine terms correctly, you would use the operator OR with the synonyms and the operator AND with different concepts. This would produce two search statements:

aspirin OR acetylsalicylic acid
heart attack OR myocardial infarction

You would then combine the two separate concepts together using AND. This would then produce relevant results, giving you items that talk about the 'use of aspirin in preventing heart attacks'.

When performing the search online, you have two choices: a simple way and a quicker, more complex way.

The simple way is to type in each of the terms above and then use a variety of ORs and ANDs to produce the desired result. Figure 2.4 shows the simple way to do this.

This search took seven steps to produce the final result. With most online services you are charged for the amount of time you are on the system, so the ideal search would be one in which you could type in a one-line search statement.

This is possible with the above search, but you must take care to ensure that the search makes sense when typed in. Boolean logic follows certain rules for combining terms using AND, OR, and NOT. Usually the AND operator is processed first, followed secondly by the OR, and then finally the NOT operator.

```
D--S/MEDL/MEDLINE 1994--NOV/P1 97(--ED970904)   SESSION   5920
COPYRIGHT BY National Library of Medicine, Bethesda MD, USA
MEDLINE 1997 IS RELOADED:   PLEASE USE MESH AND TREE 1997. SEE
BROADCAST

D--S -- SEARCH MODE -- ENTER QUERY
MEDL        1_:   aspirin

    RESULT    2668

MEDL        2_:   acetylsalicylic adj acid

    RESULT     513

MEDL        3_:   1 or 2               [Combining 1 or 2 to give total for Concept 1]

    RESULT    3091

MEDL        4_:   heart adj attack

    RESULT     179

MEDL        5_:   myocardial adj infarction

    RESULT    9529

MEDL        6_:   4 or 5               [Combining 4 or 5 to give total for Concept 2]

    RESULT    9661

MEDL        7_:   3 and 6       [Combining Concept 1 & Concept 2 to give answer]


    RESULT     467
```

Figure 2.4 *Example of search for aspirin and heart attacks*

So, looking at our analysed search, the search statement produced would be:

aspirin OR acetylsalicylic acid AND heart attack OR myocardial infarction

Now, as mentioned above, the computer would process the AND first and the ORs second. As it stands, this would produce a largely incorrect result. Why? Because the computer would be searching for aspirin OR 'the result of acetylsalicylic acid and heart attack' OR myocardial infarction.

It would, indeed, find some relevant items, but most of these would be hidden in the enormous number of non-relevant items retrieved. It would not be cost-effective to browse through these thousands of items.

How do you sort this out? Simply by the use of parentheses (or what most of us would call brackets).When 'brackets' are inserted into Boolean search statements, the computer processes what is inside the brackets first. So our one-line search statement should be typed in as:

(aspirin OR acetylsalicylic acid) AND (heart attack OR myocardial infarction)

```
D--S/MEDL/MEDLINE 1994--NOV/P1 97(--ED970904)   SESSION   5920
COPYRIGHT BY National Library of Medicine, Bethesda MD, USA
MEDLINE 1997 IS RELOADED:   PLEASE USE MESH AND TREE 1997. SEE
BROADCAST

D--S -- SEARCH MODE -- ENTER QUERY
MEDL        1_:   aspirin or acetylsalicylic adj acid and
                  heart adj attack or myocardial adj infarction

    RESULT   11764

MEDL        2_:   (aspirin or (acetylsalicylic adj acid)) and
                  ((heart adj attack) or myocardial adj
                  infarction))
```

Figure 2.5 *Entering search all in one statement*

An actual online search (Figure 2.5) shows how this works.

In reality, in most online systems, you need to add in an adjacency operator (see below) in order to search for phrases. So, the correct one-line search would be:

> (aspirin OR (acetylsalicylic ADJ acid)) AND ((heart adj attack) OR (myocardial ADJ infarction))

As Figure 2.5 shows, from the above search 11,764 items were found using the inefficient way to search, whilst only 467 were found using the efficient way. It should be obvious from this that the use of OR greatly increases the number of items retrieved and that AND reduces the number found.

In practice, however, you may wish to type in your search the simple way. It has the advantage that you don't have to retype your whole search statement if you've typed one term incorrectly. You can also very easily combine the separate terms with other terms without having to retype anything.

It all comes down to personal choice and how much time you are willing to spend online.

In the online searches above, we've used an adjacency operator 'ADJ'. We will now explain how this is used.

The adjacency operator

To be able to search for a phrase in the text of records, you need to use what is known as an adjacency operator. This is simply a tool used to tell the online system that you are searching for a phrase (not all online services require this). The term used is usually ADJ or WITH (often abbreviated to W).

To know whether to use ADJ or WITH, simply peruse the host's system manual to see what its command language uses to tell the system that it is looking for terms adjacent to each other.

When the computer processing the search strategy sees the adjacency operator it knows to search for the terms adjacent to each other, usually in the order in which you typed them.

Examples of this would be:

> heart ADJ attack
> myocardial ADJ infarction
> british ADJ library

With most systems you can say how many terms you want between the two terms you are searching for.

Examples of this would be:

> research ADJ2 development
> cats ADJ3 dogs

Truncation

So far, we've used OR to search for terms that may be synonymous to each other. In very complex searches, you may end up with between 6 and 12 terms that may need to be combined using OR. Large amounts of typing can sometimes be avoided by using what is known as truncation.

Simply put, truncation is the replacement of characters in a term by a symbol. This symbol then stands for any number of characters. The truncation character is usually either a ?

(question mark), a $ (dollar sign), or a : (colon). The piece of the term still there is called the stem.

Truncation is usually applied to the right end of the term, although some systems do allow both left and right truncation.

Suppose you were looking for literature on 'cats that have appeared in advertisements'. This search could be broken down into:

cat
cats
feline
felines

and

advert
adverts
advertisement
advertisements
advertising

If your typing wasn't fast, you could end up spending more time online than necessary. All the words beginning with the same stem could have their endings removed, and the search could be entered as:

(cat$ OR felin$) AND advert$

[the $ symbol is used as the truncation symbol, here]

That has saved us having to type in nine words. Obviously, you need to be careful where you truncate a term. Do it in the wrong place and you could end up with thousands of terms being searched and your search session being aborted.

As with the use of the adjacency operator, you can also specify, when truncating an item, the number of characters that you desire after the truncation sign.

In the above example, we would not seriously consider truncating cats to cat$ simply because using cat$ will cause the online service to look for all terms beginning with 'cat', eg catalogue, catamaran, cat, cats, catapult, cataract, cataracts, and so on.

The way around this is to indicate how many letters after the truncation symbol you require. This is very simply done, usually by using a numeric value. With cat or cats, you would use cat$1. This would find the term cat and/or cats.

Used properly truncation can save a lot of time and effort when you are online.

Summary

In this chapter we have taught you how to use the Boolean operators AND, OR, and NOT and shown how they work by using illustrations. We have explained how useful the adjacency operator is in allowing you to search for phrases in databases, and how extremely useful the truncation feature is in reducing the amount of typing in of terms in online searches.

The next chapter will teach you about the advanced search techniques that you need to know to become an effective online searcher.

Chapter 3
Advanced search techniques

Introduction

In this chapter you will learn how to be more specific in your way of searching. You will be shown how to use descriptors and their associated subheadings to retrieve relevant items.

We shall also discuss how to use field qualifiers to restrict your searches to certain fields, eg title, abstract, and so on. We will then go on to show you how you can then limit what you have found, eg by language, year of publication, and so on. All of the above will help to ensure that you find exactly what you want.

Free text vs. controlled terms

When you approach searching for the first time, you often think that you can find anything you require by typing in a couple of words you know. This may well retrieve some relevant items, but could miss hundreds of items whose authors have used terms that are different from those you would use yourself.

The reason for this is fairly obvious: we are all individuals and we choose the terms that we know, perhaps from when we studied a particular topic at degree level many, many years ago. We tend to stick to the terms that we were educated with, which may no longer be the terms used today.

To get around this problem, most databases use terms known as descriptors. These descriptors are controlled terms: that is, the same term is always used to describe the same topic, no matter what the authors have actually used.

As mentioned in Chapter 1, these descriptors are usually collected together in the form of a thesaurus, by use of which the people indexing the journal articles, or whatever, can assign the correct terms.

One disadvantage of using controlled terms is that they may not fully reflect a new term that has recently come into use. Many new words appear in the media every day, and no thesaurus that is published yearly or even quarterly is going to be bang up to date.

So, the advice for searchers is to use descriptors, where possible, and to use free text, ie words you think likely to appear in the item, for newer concepts or where a descriptor search finds no relevant items.

Descriptors

As we've said, descriptors are terms that have been chosen as the correct term to use when searching for a particular concept. For example, in the MEDLINE database, 'myocardial infarction' is used in place of 'heart attack'.

Figure 3.1 shows a search using both terms to illustrate the different numbers of items each term would find.

```
D-S/MEDL/MEDLINE 1996-OCT.'99 (-ED990812)    SESSION  6194
COPYRIGHT BY National Library of Medicine, Bethesda MD, USA

D-S - SEARCH MODE - ENTER QUERY
MEDL    1_:  heart adj attack$1                 [free text approach]

    RESULT       287

MEDL    2_:  myocardial-infarction.de.   [using MeSH descriptor term]

    RESULT      9352
```

Figure 3.1 *Free text vs. controlled terms*

Descriptors can also help in broadening or narrowing searches. Most thesauri are of the hierarchical type, whereby you look up a term and the thesaurus gives you any narrower term(s) to consider as well as broader term(s).

Staying with the MEDLINE database and using its MeSH thesaurus, we can see that looking up eye diseases in the tree structure gives you hundreds of narrower terms, ie all the specific eye diseases and a broader term for diseases.

You must be careful how you use descriptors, because inappropriate use can produce either no items or too many. Quite often the thesaurus concerned will give a small scope-note to explain the use of the term and when it came into use.

It is no good searching just on the term eye diseases, if what you wanted was a search on all types of eye disease. Most indexers tend to index very specifically, ie they will assign the most specific term they can find to a topic. An item assigned the descriptor of eye diseases will be a very general item about eye diseases.

You may want to find general items on eye diseases or very specific items on a specific eye disease, or both — everything on eye diseases. Many systems will have a function that will allow you to search for the current term and all narrower terms. In

```
D-S/MEDL/MEDLINE 1996-OCT.'99 (-ED990812)    SESSION   6194
COPYRIGHT BY National Library of Medicine, Bethesda MD, USA

D-S - SEARCH MODE - ENTER QUERY
MEDL       1_:  eye-diseases.de.

   RESULT      1415

[just searching for the term 'eye diseases']

MEDL       2_:  eye-diseases#

   RESULT      28721

[using MeSH 'explode' feature to retrieve all items about any eye disease]

[the 'explode' command in MeSH is the '#' operator]
```

Figure 3.2 *Exploded vs. unexploded term*

MEDLINE this is the 'explode' feature, an example of which is given in Figure 3.2.

Note the large difference between the unexploded and exploded term.

Sometimes these descriptors (subject headings) have sub-headings that may be applied directly to the descriptor to help narrow down your search or make it more specific.

There are over 40 subheadings used in the MEDLINE database, but not all of them are applicable to all descriptors.

Examples of subheadings that can be used in the MEDLINE database are:

adverse effects (ae)
diagnosis (di)
drug therapy (dt)
etiology (et)
occurrence (oc)
organization & administration (og)
therapy (th)

```
D-S/MEDL/MEDLINE 1996-OCT.'99 (-ED990812)    SESSION   6194
COPYRIGHT BY National Library of Medicine, Bethesda MD, USA

D-S - SEARCH MODE - ENTER QUERY
MEDL        1_:  minoxidil-ae     [adverse effects of minoxidil]

    RESULT          9


MEDL        2_:  family-practice-og     [organisation and administration
                                         of general practice]

    RESULT          610
```

Figure 3.3 *Use of subheadings*

Figure 3.3 shows examples of subheadings being used.

Descriptors usually have special ways in which they must be entered into a search in order for the search system to recognize that they are descriptors. Using Data-Star you can use .de.; DIALOG uses /de. It varies from system to system. To know which to use, consult the host's system manual and specific database information sheet.

You can now use descriptors, but how do you know that what you have searched for is a major part of the article retrieved? The answer is fairly simple. When the indexers are assigning terms, they look to see what is the main, or major, topic(s) of the paper in question. These are usually marked in some way, so that the search system knows which are major or minor terms.

Note that not all databases will use major and minor terms. In many cases there will be no distinction between the terms used to index a document. All may be of equal relevancy.

However, when searching databases that do index using this policy, to be precise, it is best to use the major terms when searching for relevant papers. Not only do you get exactly what you want, but you avoid retrieving hundreds, possibly thousands, of irrelevant items. When searching databases in Data-Star that use this facility, you can identify major search terms by using the .mj. function. See Figure 3.4 for an example.

```
D-S/MEDL/MEDLINE 1996-OCT.'99 (-ED990812)     SESSION   6194
COPYRIGHT BY National Library of Medicine, Bethesda MD, USA

D-S - SEARCH MODE - ENTER QUERY

MEDL        1_:   fetal-alcohol-syndrome.de. [your basic MeSH term]

     RESULT      327

MEDL        2_:   fetal-alcohol-syndrome.mj. [MeSH term as a major
                                              part of the article]


     RESULT      259
```

Figure 3.4 *Restricting search to major topic*

Field qualifiers

These are usually used when you either wish to restrict your search to specific fields or have found no items when using the descriptors (the subject terms used may be too new to have a thesaurus entry).

There are many fields that may be subject to qualification. Some of the more useful ones are: author, title, abstract, source, institution, language, publication years, etc. In fact, in most cases, all fields contained in a database record can be used to qualify searches to specific fields. Some may also be used in limiting, which we'll mention shortly.

How is a field qualifier used? Very simply. You would normally enter it at the end of the term you are searching for:

    Advertisement.ti.   [ti stands for title]
    word processing.ab. [ab stands for abstract]
    sri lanka/cp   [cp stands for country of publication]

Usually the information sheets about each database, eg the blue sheets in DIALOG, will contain a list of the fields and the abbreviations to use when entering your search into the computer.

You can also combine the field qualifiers, so that you could look for the same term in multiple fields. The most common combination is to search for a term that appears in both the title and abstract fields. Since abstracts are often written by the author, they should contain important terms.

Combining field qualifiers is a simple matter of putting a comma between them: see Figure 3.5

```
D-S/MEDL/MEDLINE 1996-OCT.'99 (-ED990812)    SESSION  6194
COPYRIGHT BY National Library of Medicine, Bethesda MD, USA

D-S - SEARCH MODE - ENTER QUERY
MEDL         1_:  heart adj attack$1.ti.

     RESULT       105

MEDL         2_:  heart adj attack$1.ti,ab.

     RESULT       287

MEDL         3_:  general adj pract$.ti.

     RESULT       2164

MEDL         4_:  general adj pract$.ti,ab.

     RESULT       5083
```

Figure 3.5 *Use of field qualifiers*

Limiting searches

Say you have carried out a search and have found over 500 items. You've been specific in your searching and followed most of what's been said above. You don't really want to read through all 500 items to perhaps find the 20 or 30 you require. How can you reduce these further?

The answer is rather straightforward: you can use the limit function available on most database host systems.

Most systems allow you to limit by year, language, publication type, age, animal, human, male, female, and many other database-specific limits. For example, you may be able to restrict your search to information on companies with a turnover greater than £20 million.

Limiting varies from system to system, but the principles remain the same. You first have to perform your search and then apply the limits to your answer set.

```
D-S - SEARCH MODE - ENTER QUERY
MEDL     25_:  ..limit help

MEDL: THE FOLLOWING LIMIT PARAGRAPHS ARE AVAILABLE:
R          Review Y/N                  01 ALPHA CHARACTER
REVIEW     Review Y/N                  01 ALPHA CHARACTER
AB         Abstract Y/N                01 ALPHA CHARACTER
LG         Language                    02 ALPHA CHARACTERS
YEAR       Publication year YYYY       04 NUMERIC CHARACTERS
YR         Publication year YY         02 NUMERIC CHARACTERS
IMONTH     Index Medicus mnth YYYYMM   06 NUMERIC CHARACTERS
IM         Index Medicus month YYMM    04 NUMERIC CHARACTERS
A          Animal Y/N                  01 ALPHA CHARACTER
ANIMAL     Animal Y/N                  01 ALPHA CHARACTER
M          Male (Y/N)                  01 ALPHA CHARACTER
MALE       Male (Y/N)                  01 ALPHA CHARACTER
F          Female (Y/N)                01 ALPHA CHARACTER
FEMALE     Female (Y/N)                01 ALPHA CHARACTER
H          Human Y/N                   01 ALPHA CHARACTER
HUMAN      Human Y/N                   01 ALPHA CHARACTER
C          Child Y/N                   01 ALPHA CHARACTER
CHILD      Child Y/N                   01 ALPHA CHARACTER
ADULT      Adult Y/N                   01 ALPHA CHARACTER
EDATE      NLM entry date YYYYMMDD     08 NUMERIC CHARACTERS
ED         NLM entry date YYMMDD       06 NUMERIC CHARACTERS
UDATE      Update date YYYYMMDD        08 NUMERIC CHARACTERS
UD         Update date YYMMDD          06 NUMERIC CHARACTERS
UMONTH     Update month YYYYMM         06 NUMERIC CHARACTERS
UP         Update month YYMM           04 NUMERIC CHARACTERS

D-S - LIMIT MODE - ENTER QUERY
```

Figure 3.6 *Example of the ..limit command*

But how do you know what limits to use? Once again, you can refer to the database guidance sheets or, on most systems, you can ask online.

On Data-Star, for example, typing in ..limit help will produce a list of limits that may be applied to the database you are currently using and instructions on how to type them in (see Figure 3.6).

Most people tend to use rather obvious limits, such as English language, a range of years, review articles, articles with abstracts, items concerning humans. You simply need to choose which is right for you.

```
D-S/MEDL/MEDLINE 1996-OCT.'99 (-ED990812)    SESSION  6194
COPYRIGHT BY National Library of Medicine, Bethesda MD, USA

D-S - SEARCH MODE - ENTER QUERY
MEDL        1_:  general adj pract$.ti,ab.

    RESULT     5083

MEDL        2_:  ..1/1 lg=en              [limit items found to English language]

    RESULT     4143

MEDL        3_:  ..1/2 yr gt 98 [limit items found to those from 1999 onwards]

    RESULT     440

MEDL        4_:  ..1/3 ab=y               [limit items found to those with abstracts]


    RESULT     371
```

Figure 3.7 *Use of limiting*

During limiting, you may suddenly find that the last limit you applied produced a set with no results at all. This is certainly possible, as applying successive limits may indeed result in no references. Simply go back to the last set that produced hits and display them.

Figure 3.7 shows how to apply limits on a sample Data-Star search.

SDI and saving search strategies

SDI stands for selective dissemination of information, and is usually applied to lists produced, on the user's behalf, to update the user on new items that may have appeared since the database was last updated.

It is possible for users to set up their own SDI searches, so that every time that the relevant database is updated the user is presented with new references matching their requirements. This can be done quite simply, by saving your search strategy as an SDI search (most online systems can give you a choice between saving a search strategy and saving an SDI search strategy) and then re-executing it when the new data has been added.

Because the search strategy has been saved as an SDI search, the system knows that it needs to be limited to new items only. You won't get the same items you searched for initially. This can be very useful if you need to be kept up to date about a subject area you are studying.

You can also simply save your search strategy so that you can repeat it at another time, or because you need to carry out the same search in a different database. You do need to be careful if you are repeating the search in a different database, because the descriptors used may well be different and can cause wrong hits to occur.

Saving your search strategy is straightforward, and most systems allow you to save it temporarily for 24 hours or permanently (until deleted by you).

Summary

In this chapter you will have learnt about various advanced search techniques that can enable you to retrieve relevant documents more easily.

We have discussed using free-text terms versus controlled terms; the use of descriptors (subject headings) to make your search more precise; the use of field qualifiers and how to limit searches to specific things such as language, publication type, etc. Finally, we briefly discussed SDI (selective dissemination of information).

The next chapter discusses full-text searching and how to get the best out of it.

Chapter 4
Full-text searching

Introduction

In this chapter we are going to take a look at searching full-text databases, ie databases that contain the full text of items such as newspaper articles, legislation, business reports, and so on. Graphical material such as tables, charts, and images may also be included.

There has been a large increase in the availability of full-text databases, online and on CD-ROM, since they first began to appear in the early 1980s. One of the most comprehensive listings can be found in the directory *Fulltext Sources Online* (see p. 142 for details).

Full-text databases can be incredibly useful in tracking down more obscure references and, of course, in providing direct, timely access to a complete copy of the desired item(s).

Most of the examples in this chapter are based on FT Profile's full-text service. However, the principles they illustrate are applicable to any full-text database service.

General considerations

Note first of all that the term 'full-text' can have many different connotations. There are many inconsistencies to be found as to exactly how much of an original source may be included in a 'full-text' database.

It is important to check before you begin searching whether the full-text database will actually provide the information you require, ie are items such advertisements, letters, announcements, meetings, or calendars included? Consider the policy of the database provider regarding inclusion. Also, how up to date is the electronic version of the full-text database compared with the printed original? It may be more current or it may lag considerably behind.

Searching tips and techniques

We turn now to a list of tips and techniques to help you obtain the best possible results when searching full-text databases.

Always remember that you are likely to be dealing with vast amounts of text, much more than when searching a traditional bibliographic database.

Don't search for very common words

It is quite likely that the system you are using for your search will actually incorporate a 'stop list'. This is a list of frequently used words for which you are not allowed to search, eg this, that, done, the, and so on.

Some words may not be as common as these, but in a particular subject field, may produce millions of hits, eg research, medicine, health, and so on. Some of these terms may be retrievable when searching for phrases, eg research and development, health and safety, and so on.

Searching just on the stop words would simply retrieve an unmanageable number of hits.

Use phrases to be more specific

Searching for full-text items can be made a lot easier if you can use a phrase that either describes the topic you are searching for, or perhaps is part of the topic.

For example, in FT Profile, leaving spaces between terms means 'immediately adjacent to'. Therefore, typing in the phrase 'off road vehicles' will only find items where those three words are adjacent to each other. If you tried to type this in using AND, you would have retrieved many irrelevant items and, very likely, the word 'off' would have been rejected as being a stop word.

Be creative in your choice of search terms

Use synonyms linked with the Boolean operator OR to cover as many possible ways of describing the topic in which you are interested. Include jargon and current buzz words or phrases. These can often be productive.

The OR operator in FT Profile is the comma and is placed between words you wish to search for as synonyms: eg 'cars, automobiles' would find items on either cars or automobiles.

Use positive and negative examples

Remember that there may be both positive and negative ways of phrasing the topic in which you are interested. You should include both in your search strategy if you are to retrieve all the available relevant information.

One way is to use the NOT operator to exclude items that you know you don't want. In FT Profile, the NOT symbol is the hyphen, '-'. For example, 'Maxwell - coffee' should retrieve items on Robert Maxwell, but eliminate any possibility of finding items on Maxwell House.

Proximity operators

The use of proximity operators is essential when searching full-text databases.

Although precise details vary from system to system, and so need to be checked out before you begin, you will be allowed to specify how near/far apart search terms appear in the text.

The Boolean operator AND requires only that your terms appear in the same item. FT Profile uses the '+' symbol for the AND operator, and it will look for the occurrence of the specified terms anywhere in the document.

You are strongly advised to avoid using AND when searching full-text databases (unless there are no other options). The search terms could appear several pages apart, and items retrieved could be quite irrelevant in relation to your original search query.

The nearer the terms are to one another the more specific your search results will be.

To illustrate further: DIALOG will allow you to use the connector 'w' to specify that two words be found right next to each other. The 'w' may be qualified, with a number, to indicate how many other words you are prepared to accept between your search terms. The Data-Star system, alternatively, offers the connectors 'adj', 'with', and 'same' to specify whether search terms should appear right next to each other in the text, in the same sentence, or in the same field of the database, respectively.

In FT Profile there are three operators that allow you to specify 'closeness' of terms. These are:

1 the / (forward slash), is the 'in the same sentence operator': eg 'wine / France' will find only items that have both words in the same sentence.

2 the // (double forward slash), is the 'in the same paragraph operator': eg 'Microsoft // new products' will find only items where both terms appear in the same paragraph, in any sequence.

3 just typing in terms separated by spaces: FT Profile assumes adjacency.

Truncation and use of wild-cards

Check out in advance, and make use of, any truncation and/or wild-card facilities that the system you are searching can offer. Wild-card is simply the term used to describe the use of a specific character to take the place of one or more characters when searching. This will become clearer in the examples shown below.

Truncation and/or wild-card facilities vary from system to system. They may include right-hand truncation, left-hand truncation, a mandatory wild-card facility, or an optional wild-card facility.

Right-hand truncation provides the opportunity to search for an initial word stem with any number of characters following. The OVID Technologies host system uses a $ symbol as a truncation command. With systems such as OVID's you may also specify exactly how many characters you are prepared to accept following your initial word stem.

Be very careful how far you cut back your initial word stem. Too far, ie selecting an initial word stem such as 'un' or 'an', will retrieve far too much material, mostly irrelevant in terms of your initial search query.

FT Profile uses only right-hand truncation, and this is done by means of the asterisk symbol, *. You can also specify how many additional letters after the asterisk are required: eg telecomm*, indust*5.

Left-hand truncation is offered far less often than right-hand truncation, and tends to be database specific. It provides the opportunity to search for a final word stem with any number of characters preceding it.

Again, be very careful how far you cut back your final word stem. Too far, and you will retrieve far too much material, mostly irrelevant in terms of your initial search query.

Using a *mandatory wild-card character* allows you to specify that any character appear at that point in your search term.

The OVID Technologies host system permits '#' as a mandatory wild card character. You may search, for example, for 'wom#n' to retrieve items containing the word 'women' or 'woman'. For this to work, a character must appear in the position denoted by the '#'.

Using an *optional wild-card character* allows you to specify that any character, or no character, appear at that point in your search term.

The OVID Technologies host system permits '?' as an optional wild-card character. You may search, for example, for 'colo?r' to retrieve items containing the word 'colour' or 'color'. This will work whether a character appears in the position of the '?' or not.

Singular and plural spelling

Make sure that your search strategy will retrieve both the singular and plural forms of the topic in which you are interested. Right-hand truncation and wild-card characters can be very useful tools to employ here.

Some systems, such as Data-Star, will allow you to use a function to 'set plurals on', so that typing in the singular form of a term will also retrieve the plural form.

American vs. British spelling

Make sure that your strategy will retrieve variations in spelling (within the same language of course) of any search terms that you have chosen, ie variations in British and American spelling. For example:

foetus (British)   fetus (American)
colour (British)   color (American)
aluminium (British) aluminum (American)

Wild card characters can be very useful here. Forgetting to search for a variation in spelling can mean a vast difference in the number of references retrieved.

Controlled indexing

Exploit any indexing that has been provided for the database you are searching.

Here is one instance when it may be reasonable to combine search terms with the operator AND as any indexing terms or keywords provided will be stored in a separate field of the database.

Use the indexing to search for a broad topic. Combine this with another topic, searched across the full text of the database, to narrow the focus of your search.

Exploit any field structure available for the database you are searching.

When searching FT Profile databases, for example, it is possible to specify that search terms be included only in the titles or first paragraphs of items retrieved, on the journalistic principle that all the important detail is included in the first paragraph of an article.

The relevant operators are: @HL and @START. The former is the headline operator, that instructs the system to restrict the search to the item's headlines: eg 'Thatcher@HL'. The @START operator restricts the search to the headline and the first two (text) paragraphs: eg 'John Wayne@START'.

Language enhancements

Make use of any language enhancement features that the system you are using is able to offer, eg the ability of the NEXIS system to search for singular and/or plural equivalents, British and/or American spellings, and equivalents for some compound words and common abbreviations.

New, advanced search engines may further offer 'best match' search facilities based upon complex algorithmic procedures, including linguistic and statistical methods for automatic indexing, similarity coefficients, and weighting schemes.

Speed of entry and costs

Some of the full-text databases are expensive to use and will charge for both the time online and the number of lines printed and/or downloaded.

As with any search, if you type in the individual search terms one at a time, you are likely to run up a higher charge than if you had typed your whole search strategy in at one go.

The latter method usually means using brackets around terms to indicate the order in which they should be searched for.

FT Profile is no different, but you can only use certain operators within the brackets. These are: the comma, /, //, and *. For example:

(parliament, session)@HL

would retrieve items that have either of the two words in the headline;

wine / (France, French)

would give items where wine and either France or French appear in the same sentence.

Viewing, printing, and saving results

Be very careful when displaying, printing, or saving the results of an online search.

Displaying the results of a series of full-text articles can take a lot longer and can prove a lot more expensive than displaying an equivalent number of items from a traditional bibliographic database. You could easily find yourself with a much higher search bill than expected. Check out costs and pricing policy very carefully beforehand.

When searching some systems eg DIALOG or Data-Star, you may be charged per item for full-text articles. When searching others eg FT Profile, you may be charged per line of text.

Some systems offer keyword in context (kwic) facilities when viewing search results. This means that the keywords (search terms entered) will be highlighted in the text, eg by being shown in upper case, so that you are aware of the context in which the term(s) have appeared.

You may view just a short section of the full-text items you have retrieved, containing your search terms, and from there may decide whether you wish to go on to view the item in full or not. The Data-Star system, for example, uses the commands 'kwic' and 'hits' to provide this facility. The FT Profile system uses the command 'ctx'.

Systems that are more advanced can count how frequently your search term(s) have appeared in full-text items and rank your search results accordingly. The Data-Star system, for example, uses the command '..rank' to provide this facility.

Where an intermediary, eg OVID Technologies, owns rights to both bibliographic databases and full-text sources, links may be created between these. End-users with access to the appropriate databases may, for instance, move from a search carried out in a traditional bibliographic database, such as MEDLINE, to a copy of the full article contained in a single, full-text database, such as the *New England Journal of Medicine*, and vice versa.

Search operators for FT Profile

There are numerous full-text databases available from many online hosts, eg LEXIS-NEXIS, and they will all have their own way (command language) of searching for items in the databases they host. It is outside the scope of this publication to list all the search operators of every full-text system. Please consult the relevant system's host guide on what symbols, or commands, to use.

However, FT Profile is a widely used host of full-text information. All of the FT Profile search operators are listed in Table 4.1 to help you remember them and know what they do.

Table 4.1 *FT Profile search operators*

Search operator	Usage
space	One or more spaces between terms means 'immediately adjacent to'
+	The AND operator, used to find the occurrence of two, or more terms in the same document
-	The NOT operator, used to find those items that mention one term and not the other
,	The OR opertor, used to link synonyms together
*	The TRUNCATE operator, used to search for all terms that begin with the same stem
@HL	The HEADLINE operator, used to restrict searches to the headline of an item
@START	The START operator, used to restrict searches to the headline and the first two text paragraphs
/	The IN THE SAME SENTENCE operator
//	The IN THE SAME PARAGRAPH
( )	Brackets enable you to apply search operators to more than one search term

Summary

In this chapter you learned all about full-text searching and how to find what you want by using our searching tips. Full-text searching can be more difficult than searching traditional bibliographic databases because there is so much more text.

You need to keep in mind not to search for very common words, to use phrases to be more specific, to be creative in your choice of search terms, to use both positive and negative examples, to use proximity operators, to use truncation and wild-cards, to cover singular, plural, and differences in spelling, to exploit any controlled indexing used, and to limit to specific fields.

You also need to bear in mind how much such a search will cost and whether you are paying a flat fee for access or whether you also have to pay a per-line charge for displaying or printing what you have retrieved.

The next chapter deals with searching on the Internet and very briefly shows how traditional online hosts, such as DIALOG, have transplanted themselves onto the Web. We then look at the search engines available over the Internet and how these work.

Chapter 5
Basic Internet searching

Introduction

The growth of the Internet has been phenomenal, particularly since 1993 with the introduction of the world wide web as a user-friendly, graphical interface to Internet resources. The Internet now links more than 22,000 networks in over 90 different countries. The web has established itself as a highly important, if not an essential, source of information in online searching.

In this chapter, we will first consider steps taken by traditional commercial online hosts to make use of the Internet.

We will then consider an increasing range of web search engines and subject portals. These are web-based programs, nearly all freely accessible, which have been developed to help locate material from among the sprawling, and largely unordered, 'network of networks' which goes to make up the Internet. The material itself is, by now, notorious both in terms of subject scope and quality.

As very few Internet resources are not now available via the web, the latter will be used synonymously with the term Internet throughout the rest of this chapter.

Internet-based online host systems

Many of the traditional online host services have gone on to offer web access to their systems.

In doing this, they have carried over as many search facilities as possible from their traditional dial-up services and, of course, have been able to add a Windows-based, graphical interface to these services.

Figures 5.1 and 5.2 illustrate web access to both the DIALOG and Data-Star systems.

DIALOG's home page is **http://www.dialog.com** (Figure 5.1) and Data-Star's is **http://www.datastarweb.com** (Figure 5.2).

Other host services have followed suit: the contact details for the major host systems plus either their home page or their web search page are listed in Appendix 4.

However, not all of the web hosts utilize only a web based approach. Some, like FT Profile and Ovid Technologies, have developed a client/server approach and supply their own software for Internet access (see Figures 5.3 and 5.4). In this case the user installs a special 'client' program on their own machine which connects to the host's 'server' machine.

Quite often these work quicker than traditional web pages because the majority of processing is done at the client end, ie the PC. All the server does is perform the search and send back a string of text. The PC then reformats this string of text and redraws any fancy graphics.

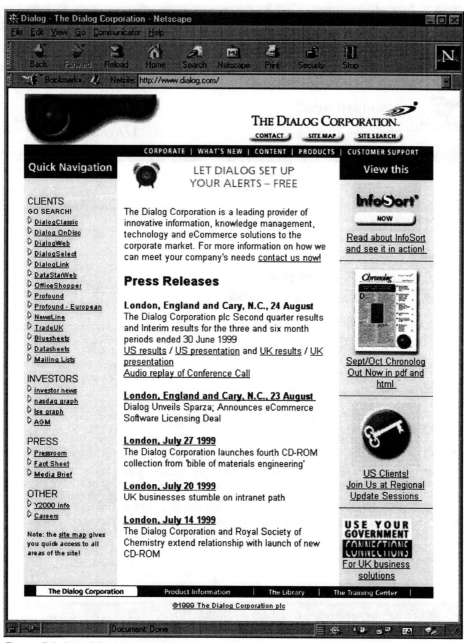

Figure 5.1 *DIALOG's home page*

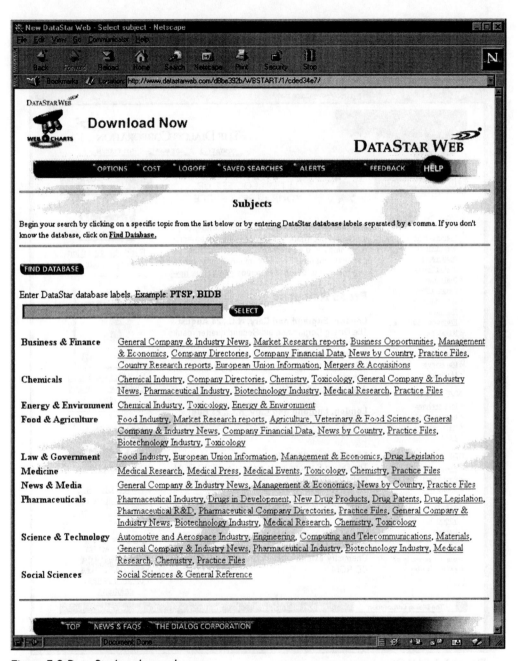

Figure 5.2 *Data-Star's web search page*

Web searches can take longer to process than client/server searches because the web page itself may need to be regenerated each time the searcher enters a search and presses the submit button.

Certain client/server programs, eg the Grateful Med program used to access the National Library of Medicine's database services, act as 'offline readers'. In this case search strategies are prepared offline. When ready, the client program connects to the host, the search request is processed, the results are brought back to the client machine and the connection is ended.

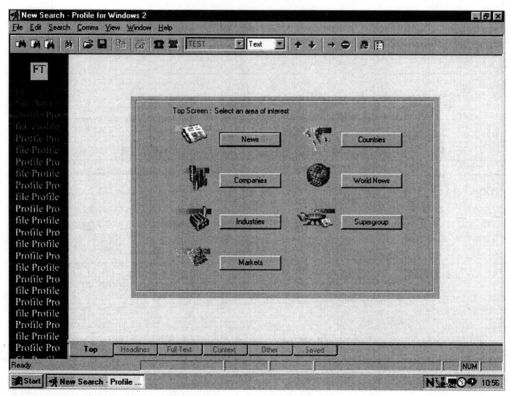

Figure 5.3 FT Profile's client/server software

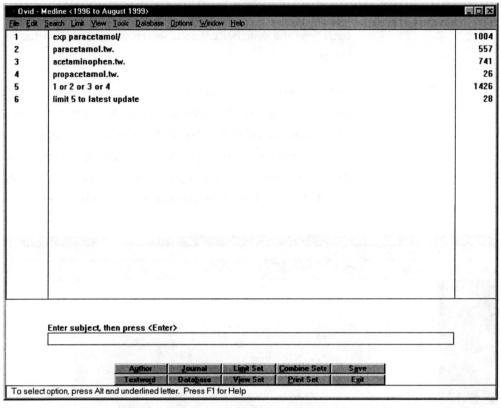

Figure 5.4 *Ovid Technology's client/server software*

This approach can be helpful for those new to online searching:

- First, as a means of being able to collect their thoughts together in order to prepare an appropriate strategy offline, and

- second, as a way of keeping online costs to a minimum.

Alternatively, searchers may prefer to remain online, interacting with the host system throughout the entire search process. This may cost more money, but you are not downloading lots of irrelevant items if you have got the search strategy wrong. It only takes one typing error and the whole search will produce either too much information, eg typing in OR instead of AND, or no information if you have spelt a term incorrectly.

The search techniques described in previous chapters are still applicable to either web based searching or using the client/ server approach. You still need to use Boolean operators and still need to think about adjacency, truncation, limiting, and so on, as used for traditional online host searching.

But traditional online host searching is not always what is required to satisfy a request for information. Databases are often not completely up to date and most of them will certainly not be full-text.

Performing a search on the web will give you access to an enormous array of information and resources on any topic imaginable. The information is often up to date and is presented in a very readable way. It is usually free, although some sites are requesting that people register with them and use an ID and password to access them.

Traditional online databases usually contain information that the creators have decided merits inclusion and may miss other useful information that has never been published in print form.

The next sections give a broad overview of what you can use to search the web in order to find sites that are useful.

Searching the web

We turn now to web search engines. These may be broadly categorized into three main types: keyword, directory, and meta-search engines. Subject portals, which are a form of meta-search engine dealing with particular subject areas, will be discussed at the end of this section.

Keyword search engines

Keyword search engines use special 'robot' programs to copy back to the main server, and index, the contents of web pages. Robot programs extract the addresses of web pages from those already indexed, and go on to add these pages to the search engine's main database(s), ever increasing the range of material covered.

One particular problem here is the one-way nature of these links. The parent web page providing the link(s) acts as a pointer only. It has no knowledge of the link page itself, should this move or become seriously out of date.

Precisely how much of each page is indexed, and to what level addresses extracted from web pages are followed up, varies from one keyword search engine to the next.

All provide keyword access to the enormous database(s) generated by the search engines' robot programs, making them particularly adept in answering the most obscure of queries.

Best results are to be achieved by using less commonly used words, words with very specific meanings, or specific phrases, when submitting search requests.

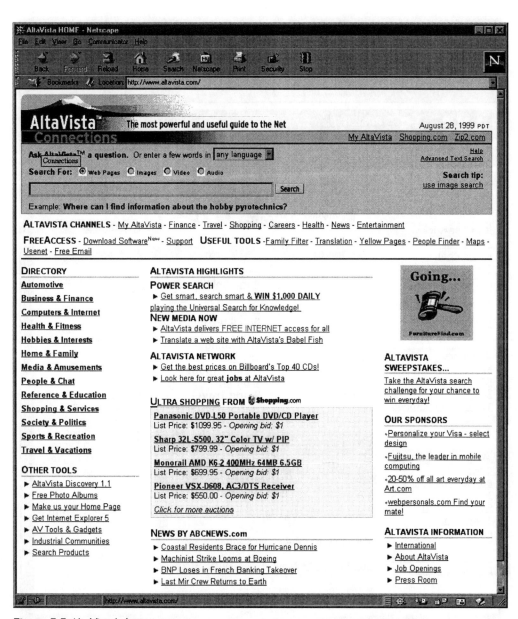

Figure 5.5 *AltaVista's home page*

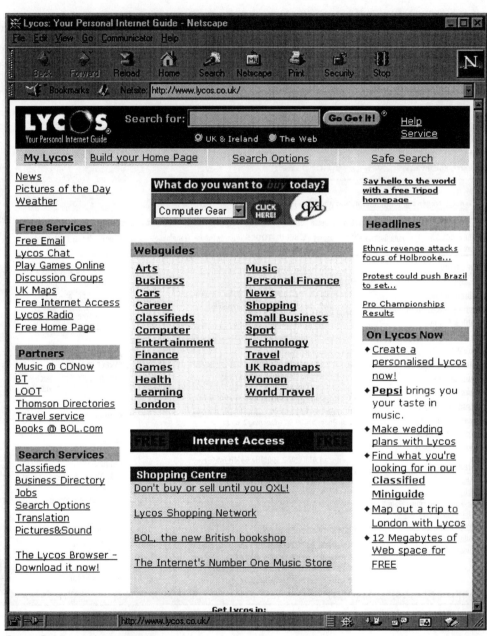

Figure 5.6 *Lycos' home page*

Two popular examples of robot search engines are AltaVista, **http://www.altavista.com** and Lycos, **http://www.lycos.com** (Figure 5.5 and 5.6 respectively).

Keyword search engines typically offer both a very simple search interface and a more advanced one.

The simple one is very easy to use, being usually a matter of typing in a few words in the search box. The search engine then looks for relevant pages by linking the terms together using the Boolean operator OR, ie the search engine looks for items where any of the terms occurs.

Keyword search engines typically use some form of relevancy ranking when displaying results. Results may be listed, for instance, according to how frequently search terms appear in the item, the placement of terms within an item, or even a site's popularity.

Poor ranking algorithms, as well as the sheer amount of material now indexed, are important reasons why so many complain of the volume of material that can be retrieved using a keyword search engine.

The problem is made worse by 'index spamming' techniques used to push individual pages higher up the ranking system. These include adding frequently sought words to web pages or the excessive repeating of keywords on a web page.

If no pages are found where all terms appear, then the search engine usually lists pages for those terms it has found. However, this is likely to produce millions of irrelevant pages.

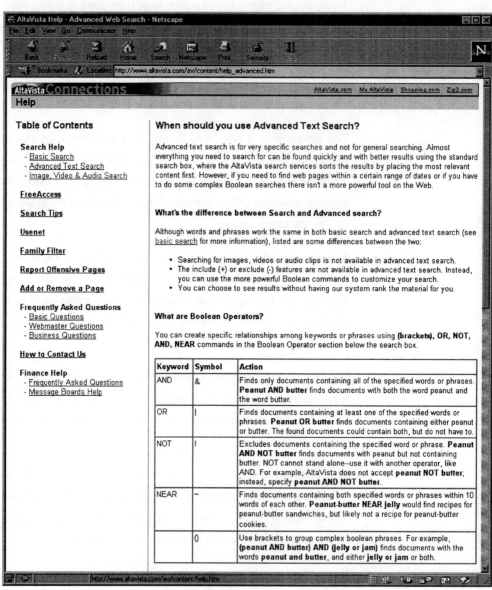

Figure 5.7 *AltaVista's help page for advanced searching*

AltaVista, for example, according to their 'About AltaVista' page (see **http://www.altavista.com/av/content/about.htm**), has a 140 million page index, with the content of those pages being refreshed every 28 days.

As more and more sites are launched, the number of pages held by a search engine will increase. No one can say reliably how many web pages are out there because the figure changes every second.

For a competent searcher, the best approach is to use the 'advanced text search'. This will, usually, allow you to use all of the Boolean operators, truncation, adjacency, and everything else that we have discussed previously.

The search engines will usually also provide additional ways of narrowing down searches. Help will usually be available on the site and will show you how to use these additional features. The help page from AltaVista (Figure 5.7) shows information on how to perform advanced text searches.

Keyword search engines do not number search sets or allow for the complex nesting of search sets. Database fields, as such, do not exist in web pages and so cannot be used to restrict your search to a particular section of each page.

AltaVista offers instead the ability to restrict a search to particular elements defined by HTML tags such as 'URL' or 'title', while Lycos offers the ability to search specifically for images or graphics. The term HTML stands for hypertext mark up language, the special form of coding used when creating, and when your web browser reads, web pages. The term URL stands for uniform resource locator, the name given to the unique address provided for each web page, eg **http://ovid.bma.org.uk** for the introductory page to the BMA Library's MEDLINE Plus service.

When using a keyword search engine it may be necessary to include any refinements in search technique with your initial search strategy. There may be no way of referring to your search results again later except by repeating the search.

With keyword search engines the very brief and/or incomplete details provided about each item in a results' display are often not enough to tell whether an item is likely to be useful or not.

Other problems that occur include speed of response (search engines being heavily used websites) and the quality of the help or search instructions provided. This can be particularly poor considering that search engines are intended as end-user tools.

However, web search engines are continuing to evolve. One of the latest is called Google and is found at **http://www.google.com** (Figures 5.8 and 5.9).

This is a new type of search engine that uses a complicated mathematical analysis, calculated on more than a billion hyperlinks on the web, to return high-quality search results so that you don't have to sift through junk.

In essence, Google interprets a link from page A to page B as a vote, by page A, for page B. Google assesses a page's importance by the votes it receives. But Google looks at more than sheer volume of votes, or links; it also analyses the page that casts the vote. Votes cast by pages that are themselves 'important' weigh more heavily and help to make other pages 'important'.

Figure 5.8 *Google's home page (Copyright 1999 Courtesy of Google, Inc.)*

Of course, the importance of a page means nothing to you unless it matches your query. So Google uses sophisticated text-matching techniques to find pages that are both important and relevant to your search. For instance, when considering a page, Google looks at what the pages linking to that page have to say about it.

If you are frustrated by other search engines, then please try Google!

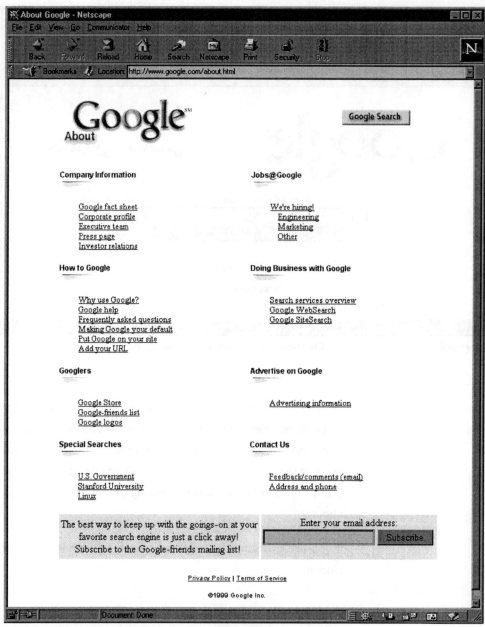

Figure 5.9 *Google's answers page (Copyright 1999 Courtesy of Google, Inc.)*

Directory search engines

Directory search engines offer hierarchical listings of Internet resources.

These are organized by human effort according to some basic underlying principle, such as a simple alphabetical listing, the Library of Congress classification scheme, and others.

Where keyword search engines have been likened to the index of a printed book, directory search engines may be likened more to a list of contents.

One of the most popular examples of a directory search engine is Yahoo! **http://www.yahoo.com** (see Figure 5.10).

Some directory search engines, such as Magellan (**http://magellan.excite.com**), go on to provide descriptions or reviews of the resources they cover (see Figure 5.11).

Such descriptions or reviews vary widely from one directory search engine to the next, but can prove extremely useful in evaluating search results.

Directory search engines can be very useful for browsing information on a particular subject, less so for natural language searching.

One of the major problems in connection with directory search engines is the reliance on people to build and maintain their content. This content is highly selective, as opposed to the very broad scope of keyword search engines. However, this may be an advantage where quality is one of the important selection criteria.

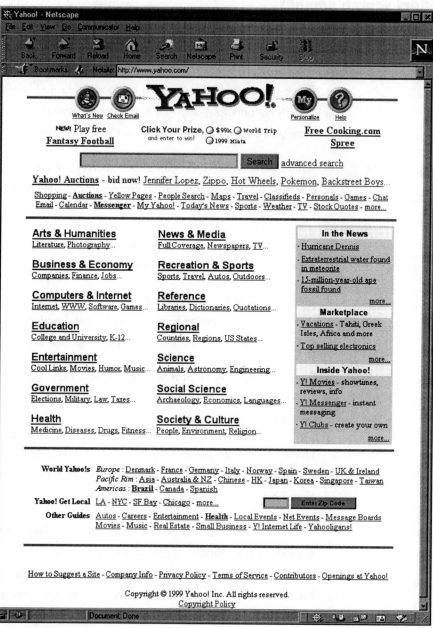

Figure 5.10 *Yahoo!'s home page*

Figure 5.11 *Magellan's page showing results of search on the word 'Internet'*

Meta-search engines

Meta-search engines are designed to access a number of other search engines simultaneously.

The main advantage here is that the searcher can be sure to have incorporated a range of approaches in seeking the information they require from the Internet.

Disadvantages include the additional time taken to perform a search, as opposed to using just a single search engine, and the necessity to formulate a search strategy that can be understood by even the simplest of the individual search engines included as part of the meta-search.

The home pages of two examples of meta-search engines, SavvySearch (**http://www.savvysearch.com**) Figure 5.12, and WebCrawler (**http://www.webcrawler.com**) Figure 5.13, are shown below.

As web resources continue to grow and search engines evolve, a skilled information worker must recognize the problems involved in searching for Internet resources and the importance of keeping up to date with new developments, even with the huge variation in quality of material available.

Skilled searchers must accept that the best they may hope to achieve at the moment is to prepare a general strategy, making full use of the range of different search engines available and the range of facilities offered by these search engines.

Figure 5.12 *SavvySearch's home page (Copyright 1999 SavvySearch Limited. All rights reserved.)*

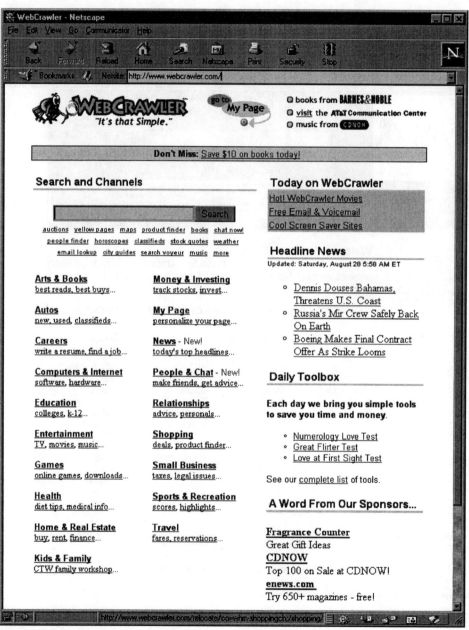

Figure 5.13 WebCrawler's home page

Subject portals

Web search engines have been developed initially by computer scientists, by borrowing techniques from information retrieval research such as best-match searching and relevance ranking.

Information professionals are increasingly bringing their skills to help organize the growing wealth of Internet resources. A good example of their influence is the development of subject-specific web search engines (subject portals), where evaluation of material covered is a major concern.

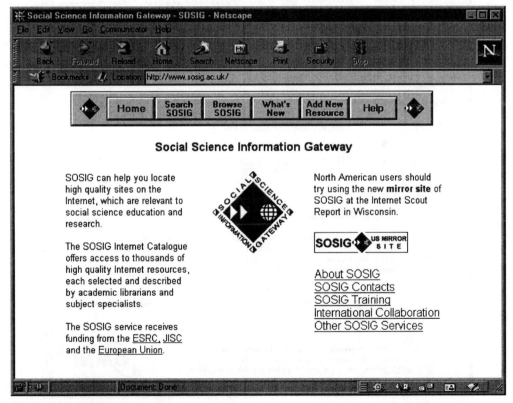

Figure 5.14 SOSIG's home page

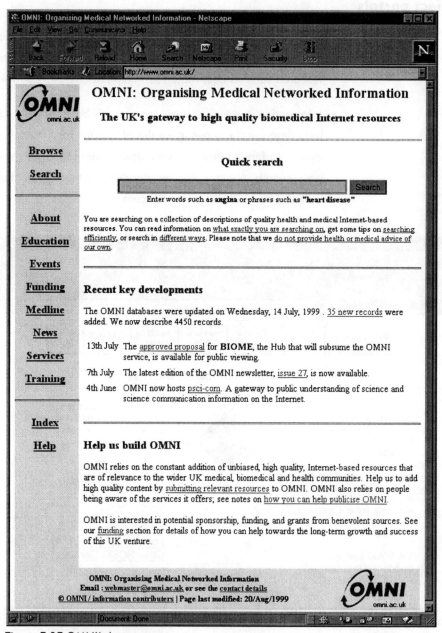

Figure 5.15 *OMNI's home page*

Two prime UK examples of subject portals are SOSIG (social science information gateway, **http://www.sosig.ac.uk**), covering social science resources, and OMNI (organizing medical networked information, **http://www.omni.ac.uk**), covering medical resources; their home pages are shown in Figures 5.14 and 5.15, respectively.

There are numerous subject portals available on the web. Some very useful ones are listed in Table 5.1.

Table 5.1 *Subject portals*

Selected subject portals	Web address
ADAM: art, design, architect and media	**http://www.adam.ac.uk**
Biz/ed: business studies and economics	**http://bized.ac.uk**
EEVL: engineering information	**http://eevl.ac.uk**
ELDIS: electronic development and environment information system	**http://nt1.ids.ac.uk/eldis**
History	**http://ihr.sas.ac.uk**
Human Language Page	**http://www.june29.com/HLP**
HUMBUL: humanities resources	**http://users.ox.ac.uk/~humbul**
OMNI: organizing medical networked information	**http://www.omni.ac.uk**
SciCentral: science resources	**http://www.scicentral.com/index.html**
SOSIG: social science information gateway	**http://www.sosig.ac.uk**

Subject portal sites can be very helpful, but they should be used with care. Users should bear in mind the following points:

- The aim of the subject portal is to list and review the most important sites on the web relevant to that subject. The sites are usually constantly peer-reviewed to ensure that the site is relevant and up to date.

- New sites are appearing all the time. Relying on a subject portal site to find everything you require may mean that you miss an important site that has recently appeared and has not yet been reviewed by the producers of the particular subject portal.

- A subject portal is a one stop shop for information on the topic it covers. You don't have to carry out extensive Internet searches in order to find the information you require. You can simply go to the subject portal site you require.

- Subject portals save you having to have long lists of bookmarks (saved addresses of web pages) which are often cumbersome and time-consuming to arrange and keep up to date. However, if you do prefer to use bookmarks you can arrange them in an order to suit the way you work and not have an order forced on you by the subject portal.

- A subject portal site is only as good as the reviewers who peer-review the sites listed. The reviewers need to have a policy of keeping the portal sites up to date and of constantly reviewing the sites they list, to make sure that they are still relevant and still contain good, timely information.

- A subject portal may be available to everyone who needs to use it or to only certain groups of users. A good portal should be publicly available to anyone who needs it.

Summary

First of all we looked briefly at how traditional online services had transformed themselves into Internet-based online services using web-based technologies. We then turned to discussing web-based search engines as a means of finding relevant pages on the Internet.

We talked about keyword search engines, directory search engines, meta-search engines, and subject portals. Each type could be used in a different way, from simple keyword searching up to peer-reviewed web sites. Ten of the more well known subject portal sites available on the web were listed.

The next chapter looks at ways and means of improving quantity and quality (recall and precision) in your searches.

Chapter 6
Quantity vs. quality (recall vs. precision)

Introduction

The effectiveness of an online search may be measured both in terms of recall (the quantity of material retrieved) and precision (the quality, or relevance, of the material retrieved).

These two measures work in inverse proportion to one another.

To broaden your search, in an attempt to retrieve more material, increases the likelihood of retrieving some irrelevant material.

To narrow the focus of your search, in an attempt to maximize the relevance of your search results, increases the likelihood that some relevant material may be missed.

A good search strategy is one which achieves an appropriate balance between the two measures of recall and precision.

In this chapter we aim to bring together a list of tips and techniques discussed earlier to act as a checklist in helping to improve both the recall and precision of your search strategies.

Improving the recall of your search strategy

As mentioned above, recall is a measure of how many items have been retrieved, the aim being to find as much information as possible. Recall is usually measured against how many items are out there in the universe of the literature, but it is usually very difficult to know how many papers on a certain topic there are.

To improve the numbers of references found, we would suggest the following approaches:

1   Use all the necessary search tools to list as many synonyms as possible for each search term. Consult as many thesauri as possible and think what terms other people would use. Then use truncation in order to cut down on the typing. For example, when searching for 'cat' we can use CAT$1, FELINE$1, the Latin name, and any and all variants in other languages, eg Felius Cattus, Gatto, and so on.

2   Don't restrict a search to any specific language or any other database-specific limit. If you have done so, go back to the set that was there before limiting was used.

There may well be a significant minority of core journal articles (or even web pages) that exist only in a foreign language. If the aim is to retrieve all relevant information, then these are relevant. You can always have the papers translated.

3   Search over the whole of each record held within the database. Use both descriptors and free text searching.

Sometimes indexers don't apply the correct term(s) when indexing an item, or can't decide, for example in medicine, whether the paper is a clinical trial, a review or whatever.

4   Use the 'explode' function where possible. The explode function is MEDLINE's terminology, and it will enable you to retrieve all the items on your topic plus all the items on topics considered to be narrower terms than those you are searching for.

Not all terms will have narrower ones, but you could easily miss hundreds, if not thousands, of relevant items if you don't use this feature.

For example, searching for items on 'complications in eye diseases' will retrieve more items if the term 'eye disease' is exploded.

5   Try not to use the Boolean operator NOT as this may well exclude useful references.

Quite often researchers will write papers dealing with two dissimilar topics, or comparing two different types of drugs. For example, there will exist papers which contain discussions comparing the efficacy of two different drugs for one condition.

If you are trying to find information on one of the drugs and use NOT to exclude the other, then you are reducing the recall for the topic for which you are searching.

6   If possible, select a range of databases that contain similar subjects.

Databases produced by different organizations on the same, or similar, topics will have an overlap of journals they index for their databases, but there will also be some unique journals contained in each database.

For example, when carrying out a comprehensive search of the medical literature, it is usually best to search MEDLINE, Embase, and Biosis. They are all produced by different organizations and they all contain the same basic core journals.

However, each database concentrates on a different segment of the medical/biological field and the overlap between each is about 50-60%, ie about 40-50% of items in each database are unique to that database.

Performing a search in one database only may seriously cut down on the quantity of references retrieved.

Improving the precision of your search strategy

As mentioned above, precision (quality) is a measure of how relevant the items are that have been retrieved. Even if you find only three items out of a possible 1000, if all three are precisely what you were looking for, then your precision is 100%.

Precision is usually measured by dividing the total number of items found by the number of relevant items, and is expressed as a percentage. The aim is to obtain 100% precision (or as near as possible).

Listed below are our tips to improve the precision of a search.

1   Analyse the search topic exhaustively to ensure that you have included all relevant terms.

Some of these terms may be questionable: they may be the terms that the enquirer has used to describe the topic, though they may not be used for indexing or even appear in the thesaurus. However, they will be useful for making the search more precise.

For example, we previously considered a search on the use of aspirin in preventing the risk of heart attacks. At the time, we ignored the words 'preventing' and 'risk' and concentrated on 'aspirin' and 'heart attacks'. If the original search had found hundreds of items concerning aspirin and heart attacks, then we could be more precise (narrow the search down) by 'ANDing' in the terms PREVENT$ and RISK$1.

2   Select the database that best fits your search. By the use of database guides and host system guides you should be able to decide which is the best database to search in order to obtain relevant references. You could search more than one database, but your precision is likely to go down (whilst your recall goes up).

3   Try to search using the descriptors (subject terms) that the people indexing the articles have assigned to the articles. Indexers are usually subject specialists and will have assigned the most relevant specific term that they can find.

4   Ensure that you search for the major descriptors where possible.

Whilst searching for a term in the descriptor field will produce relevant items, you will also find items where the term has been mentioned in just a paragraph or two. The indexers have included it in the list of descriptors but have applied no weighting to it.

In the MEDLINE database, for example, the indexers weight the term more heavily if it appears to be a major part of the article being indexed. These are called 'major' descriptors and the others are called 'minor' ones.

5 If necessary, use field qualifiers to narrow down the search even further.

6 Use database limits, such as language, year ranges, and so on, to again make the search more precise.

Summary

You have seen that there are certain ways and means of improving both recall and precision. As mentioned at the beginning of the chapter, any online search should be a balance between the amount of items retrieved and the relevancy of those items.

Two separate lists of ideas by which you can enhance one or the other are given above. In reality, however, when carrying out an online search, you need to combine both sets of tips.

Start off broadly and ensure that you have covered most of the literature on the requested topic. Then focus in on what the topic is about. Find papers where the topic is a major part of the article, book, or web page.

Look at how many items have been found. More than about 100 is usually too high, unless the request has been to find out everything on the topic. If too many items have been found then limit the search to specific categories, ie language, date range, type of publication (eg review articles).

The next chapter takes you through five worked examples of literature searches, using five different databases.

Chapter 7
Worked examples

Introduction

In this final chapter we will go though five online searches with you, from the receipt of the request to the printing out of relevant references.

We shall use a variety of databases and both the DIALOG host system and Data-Star (the main two that we have passwords for).

The concepts that are produced by analysing the topic may well not be as comprehensive as possible, simply because we haven't got the room or the time to go into very much depth. This is left to the reader who, we are sure, will be able to think up more synonyms and other terms.

Sample searches

A Can you find me papers on consumer attitudes to environmental problems caused by different types of industry?

B What effects do meteorite showers have on communication satellites?

C Please supply all information on the unmanned spacecraft that have visited Mars and Jupiter.

D What effect does the economic development of Third World countries have on quality of life of their populations?

E How are interlibrary loans automated by using computers?

Sample search A

Can you find me papers on consumer attitudes to environmental problems caused by different types of industry?

On first glance this produces the following concepts:

Concept 1   consumers
consumer attitudes
consumer views

Concept 2   environment
environmental pollution
environmental damage
pollution

Concept 3   industrial plants
industrial waste
industry

The next stage is to look at any thesaurus/classification schemes available whereby you can discover relevant subject descriptors to be used in the search. Then use the database guides and system host guides to decide on the database and the host.

The database we've chosen to do the search in is ABI/Inform, which covers all phases of business and management. We chose this one as it seems an appropriate one in which to discover the view of the consumer.

The host system is Data-Star, mainly because we are very familiar with the host system and because it is hosted in Switzerland rather than the USA.

Looking at the thesaurus and other guides, we feel that a free-text approach is better for this type of search. There is a heading for CONSUMER ATTITUDES and we will link this to a free-text search on ENVIRONMENT$ and INDUSTR$.

We will possibly then limit by English language and maybe by date.

Figure 7.1 shows the actual search session on Data-Star and some sample titles.

```
D--S/INFO/ABI/INFORM '71 TO DATE                    SESSION   6201
COPYRIGHT BY UMI/Data Courier, Louisville KY, USA

D--S -- SEARCH MODE -- ENTER QUERY
INFO          1_:   consumer-attitudes.de.        [Note use of .de. to qualify
                                                   term as descriptor]

       RESULT        7326

INFO          2_:   environment$                   [Note use of $ as truncation
                                                   symbol]

       RESULT    259594

INFO          3_:   industr$4

       RESULT    999530

INFO          4_:   1 and 2 and 3

       RESULT        773
```

[Too many items found, so make it more precise by limiting sets 2 & 3 to the descriptor field]

```
INFO          5_:   1 and 2.de. and 3.de.

       RESULT         20

INFO          6_:   ..p ti/1-5

          1   INFO
TI Can't see the paper for the labels.

          2   INFO
TI The environmental divide.

          3   INFO
TI Buyers' green demands challenge suppliers.

          4   INFO
TI Consumers lack awareness of environmental packaging.

          5   INFO
TI Packaging maximizes value of environmental influences.
```

Figure 7.1 *Search A*

Sample search B

What effects do meteorite showers have on communication satellites?

Analysing the search topic, we arrive at two main concepts:

Concept 1   meteorite showers
             meteorites
             meteors

Concept 2   communication satellites
             satellite communication
             communications

The search is going to take place in the Compendex database on Data-Star. It's a very useful database since it covers all areas of engineering and science and management, including mathematics, and both bibliographic and conference information is included.

After looking at the appropriate guides and resources, we'll be searching using the terms:

Satellite Communication Systems.de. AND (meteor$1 OR meteorit$2)

We may also add the free text term 'satellite communicat$4'. We're using the two separate meteor terms simply because there are other terms, such as meteorology, that we would retrieve if we just used meteor$.

Figure 7.2 shows the actual search session on Data-Star and some sample titles.

```
D--S/COMP/EI COMPENDEX (R) '76--              SESSION   6202
COPYRIGHT BY Engineering Index Inc, Hoboken NJ, USA

D--S -- SEARCH MODE -- ENTER QUERY
COMP       1_:   satellite-communication-systems.de.

    RESULT      3570

COMP       2_:  satellite adj communication$4

    RESULT      7505

COMP       3_:  1 or 2

    RESULT      7505            [Note set 2 contains all from set 1]

COMP       4_:  meteor$1

    RESULT       684

COMP       5_:  meteorite$1

    RESULT       451

COMP       6_:  4 or 5

    RESULT      1047

COMP       7_: 3 and 6

    RESULT        14

COMP       8_:  ..p ti/1-3

        1   COMP
TI Probability--temporary characteristics of the radial
networks of meteor communication.

        2   COMP
TI Proceedings of the 6th International Conference on HF
Radio Systems and Techniques.

        3   COMP
TI INTELSAT VI SSTDMA subsystem timing source oscillator
control.
```

Figure 7.2 *Search B*

Sample search C

Please supply all information on the unmanned spacecraft that have visited Mars and Jupiter.

This is fairly straightforward. We would suggest a free-text approach, because the requester wants 'all' information. This approach will search all the fields in each record, including the descriptor field.

Analysing the search topic produces the following concepts:

Concept 1	Mars
	Ares
Concept 2	Jupiter
	Jovian
Concept 3	unmanned spacecraft
	probes
	space probes

We've chosen the Inspec database for this since it corresponds to Physics Abstracts, Electrical and Electronic Abstracts, and Computer and Control Abstracts.

Since we are going to take a free-text approach, we will search for the following:

(mars OR ares OR jupiter OR jovian) AND (unmanned OR probe$1)

Figure 7.3 shows the actual search session on Data-Star and some sample titles.

```
D--S/INSP/INSPEC '87--V99:I34                SESSION  6203
COPYRIGHT BY Inst. of Electrical Engineers, Stevenage, UK

D--S -- SEARCH MODE -- ENTER QUERY
INSP      1_:   (mars or ares or jupiter or jovian
                and (unmanned or probe$1)

   RESULT      302

INSP      2_:   ..1/1 lg=en

   RESULT      291

D--S -- SEARCH MODE -- ENTER QUERY
INSP      3_:   ..p ti/1-5

      1  INSP
TI Chemistry of the Jovian auroral ionosphere.

      2  INSP
TI On the electromagnetic fields generated by a slowly moving
conducting body in a magnetized plasma. Possible applications
for the Io--Jovian system, spacecraft, and plasma probes.

      3  INSP
TI Propagation of electromagnetic waves through the Martian
ionosphere.

      4  INSP
TI Further evaluation of waves and turbulence encountered by
the Galileo Probe during descent in Jupiter's atmosphere.

      5  INSP
TI Three--dimensional boundary--value inverse heat--
conduction problem.
```

Figure 7.3 *Search C*

Sample search D

What effect does the economic development of Third World countries have on quality of life of their populations?

Reading the search statement, you immediately know that it's to do with sociology, and this means searching the Sociological Abstracts database.

Sociological Abstracts is a primary source of worldwide literature on theoretical and applied sociology and related disciplines, including: political science, policy and forecasting science, family studies, gerontology, urban and rural sociology, and feminist studies.

The topic can be broken down into the following concepts:

Concept 1   economic development
economy

Concept 2   third world countries
developing countries

Concept 3   quality of life
life style

Using the appropriate tools, we will employ the search strategy:

((quality of life.de.) OR (life adj style$) OR lifestyle$) AND economic$.de. AND developing countries.de.

If that doesn't find what we require, then we may have to use a free-text search, or even drop one of the concepts. Figure 7.4 shows the results of the search.

```
D--S/SOCA/SOCIOLOGICAL ABSTRACTS . '63--        SESSION   6204
COPYRIGHT BY Sociological Abstracts Inc, San Diego CA, USA

D--S -- SEARCH MODE -- ENTER QUERY
SOCA       1_:  quality-of-life.de.

   RESULT     1180

SOCA       2_:  life adj style$1

   RESULT      863

SOCA       3_:  lifestyle$1

   RESULT     3684

SOCA       4_:  economic$.de.

   RESULT     19082

SOCA       5_:  developing-countries.de.

   RESULT     4467

SOCA       6_:  (1 or 2 or 3) and 4 and 5

   RESULT       10

SOCA       7_:  ..p ti/1-4

        1  SOCA
TI Structural Adjustment, Safety Nets, and Destitution.

        2  SOCA
TI Foreign  Direct  Investment  and Economic Sectors: Their
Influence on the Provision of Basic Needs in Developing
Nations.

        3  SOCA
TI Economic  Disarticulation  and  Social  Development in
Less--Developed Nations: A Cross--National Study of
Intervening Structures.

        4  SOCA
TI Colonial Legacies at Twentieth Century's End.
```

Figure 7.4 *Search D*

Sample search E

How are interlibrary loans automated by using computers?

Splitting this up, just by looking at the search request, we get the following two concepts:

Concept 1   interlibrary loans
            ILL
            ILLs

Concept 2   automated
            automation
            computerised
            computerized

The phrase 'automated by computers' is really a duplication, because ILLs are always automated by using computers. There are, no doubt, more terms and/or synonyms that could be added to the above two concepts.

The thing to do next, is to look at the LISA thesaurus/classification scheme to see if there are specific indexing terms available to use for any, or all, of the concepts listed above.

In fact, there is one that takes care of both concepts with one compound term, ie 'computerized interloans'.

However, if you wanted to be absolutely sure that you had found everything, we would also suggest taking the above concepts to search File 61 on DIALOG, using the terms

inter(w)library(w)loan? AND (automat? OR comput?)

Note the use of the proximity operator 'with', w, and the use of brackets around the terms that have been 'OR'd' together.

Figure 7.5 shows the actual search session on DIALOG and some sample titles.

```
File   61:LISA(LIBRARY&INFOSCI)   1969--1999/Aug
       (c) 1999 Reed Reference Publishing

       Set   Items   Description
       ---   -----   -----------
?ss computerized interloans/de        [Use of /de to limit to descriptor field]

       S1       130   COMPUTERIZED INTERLOANS/DE
?ss inter(w)library(w)loan? and (automat? or comput?)

       S2      1709   INTER
       S3    107510   LIBRARY
       S4      5174   LOAN?
       S5       460   INTER(W)LIBRARY(W)LOAN?
       S6     13316   AUTOMAT?
       S7     47296   COMPUT?
       S8       122   INTER(W)LIBRARY(W)LOAN? AND (AUTOMAT?
              OR COMPUT?)
?ss s1 or s8

              130   S1
              122   S8
       S9      241   S1 OR S8      [Combing the descriptor and free-text search]
?ss s9/eng

       S10      152   S9/ENG        [Limiting to items in English]
?T 10/ti/1-4


 10/TI/1
CIC and OCLC transform interlibrary loan services with new
agreement.

 10/TI/2
An examination of the consequences of electronic innovations.

 10/TI/3
The day it rained in Fort Collins, Colorado.

 10/TI/4
Denver Public Library's adaptation of messaging technologies.
```

Figure 7.5 *Search E*

Summary

In this chapter we have gone through five different worked examples of types of search requests that you may receive. Approaches have varied from free-text to the use of controlled vocabulary, the use of the adjacency operator, and limiting by certain categories.

Throughout the book we have shown you various ways and means of digging out the relevant information you require, and we hope that this chapter has brought those ideas together.

Appendix 1
History of computers, online searching, and the Internet

Introduction

This appendix is included so that you can trace the development of the present-day computer and telecommunication services. It is not intended to be totally comprehensive, since much of the information can be found on the web or in textbooks. However, we've picked out what we consider to be milestones. To gather the material, we searched the web and consulted various textbooks. The major sources used are listed at the end of this appendix.

History

1791

Charles Babbage, the 'father of computing', is born.

1819

Hans C. Oersted discovers that a wire carrying an electric current deflects a magnetic needle; this eventually leads to the creation of the telegraph.

1837

William F. Cooke and Charles Wheatstone install the first railway telegraph in England.

1844

Samuel F. B. Morse demonstrates a magnetic telegraph using his Morse code to send the message 'What hath God wrought' from Baltimore to Washington.

1876

Alexander Graham Bell transmits the first message ever sent by telephone, 'Mr. Watson, come here, I want you', to his assistant, linked by wire and receiver to the sending device in Bell's office.

1877

The world's first commercial telephone is introduced and the first telephone line is installed between Charlie Williams' electrical shop on Court Street, Boston, and his home, three miles away.

1895

Guglielmo Marconi transmits the first signal via electromagnetic waves: radio transmission is born.

1901

Marconi receives the first ever electromagnetic wave signal from across the Atlantic on 12th December.

1939

The first electronic digital computer, the Atanasoff-Berry Computer, is created with a $7000 grant at Iowa State University by John Vincent Atanasoff and Clifford Berry.

1947

John Bardeen, William Shockley, and Walter Brattain invent the transistor, whilst at Bell Labs. They receive the Nobel prize in physics in 1956 for their work.

1956

The first hard-disk drive is born at IBM. It is the size of two large refrigerators and holds 5Mb of data at a cost of $10,000 per Mb.

1957

The USSR launches Sputnik, the first artificial satellite.

1960

The first communications satellite, Echo, is launched.

1962

AT&T places the first commercial communications satellite (Telstar 1) in orbit.

The TIP (Technical Information Project) is carried out at MIT from 1962, designed as a test-bed for the evaluation of computerized libraries and scientific communications. The project uses an IBM 7094 and contains 35,000 articles from 25 physics journals. Searching is performed using keywords, titles, and bibliographic coupling for similar papers.

1963

MARC (machine readable catalogue) is suggested in a report on the development of the Library of Congress.

MEDLARS (medical literature analysis and retrieval system) is formed following three years of design work at the National Library of Medicine (NLM). Public service starts in 1966.

1964

Digital Equipment Corporation (DEC) releases its PDP-8 computer, the first mass-produced minicomputer.

RAND's Paul Baran publishes 'On distributed communications networks', which outlines packet-switching networks.

The American Library Association gives the first public demonstration of online searching at the 1964 New York's World's Fair. The Library USA exhibition has a link to a UNIVAC 490 with 'fastrad' direct-access drum memory. Six terminals are able to search interactively the W. H. Wilson 'Reader's Guide'.

Lockheed Missiles Corporation (forerunner of DIALOG) demonstrates an online system, known as CONVERSE, to search its in-house library system.

1965

Thomas Merrill and Lawrence Roberts set up the first wide area network (WAN) between MIT's Lincoln Lab and System Development Corporation (SDC).

Estimates suggest that there are between 12 and 20 machine bibliographic databases in existence.

Hal Borko announces the BOLD (bibliographic online display) system, which uses Boolean algebra for searching and ranks output according to the number of hits scored against the search strategy.

The first commercial SDI (selective dissemination of information) service, ASCA (automatic subject citation alert), is run by the Institute of Scientific Information.

Chemical Abstracts starts to issue part of its abstracts data as magnetic tape.

SDC, in a project funded by ARPA (Advanced Research Projects Agency), is involved in developing a system that allows 13 government and private organizations access, via a telephone, to a file of 200,000 bibliographic records on foreign technology.

1966

Scientists use fibre optics to carry telephone signals for the first time.

MEDLARS is officially launched to the general public.

IBM begins development of the forerunner of STAIRS (storage and information retrieval system) for in-house use.

1967

OCLC (Ohio Colleges Library Centre) is founded with 48 member libraries.

Experimental facsimile (fax) transmission service is set up by New York State Library to connect 15 sites. However, transmissions peak at only 30 requests per day and the service is closed in 1968.

1968

The first WAN to use packet switching is tested at the National Research Laboratory (NRL) in the UK.

The first regular online catalogue for users is started by the State University of New York (SUNY) Medical Research Library Downstate Medical Centre.

1969

The RIOT (retrieval of information by online terminal) system is developed at the Culham Laboratory of the UKAEA (UK Atomic Energy Authority) for searching legal documents. The system is based on earlier research that had provided a regular computer-based SDI system from April 1966.

OSTI (the Office for Scientific and Technical Information) finances two experiments investigating the potential for library cooperation in the field of automation: the Birmingham Libraries Cooperative Mechanization Project deals with cooperative cataloguing, and SWALCAP (the South West Area Library Cooperative Automation Project), set up between the universities of Bristol, Cardiff, and Exeter, concentrates initially on circulation.

The Space Documentation Centre of the European Space Agency (ESA) acquires RECON (remote console) from the USA and begins an online information service, covering several databases, to 10 terminals in seven European countries.

At the NLM, the Abridged Index Medicus by Teletypewriter Exchange Network (AIM/TWX) provides access, via SDC and the telephone network, to 100 journals in clinical medicine. Within six months, 90 institutions are using it.

1971

The ORBIT (online retrieval of bibliographic information time-shared) system, developed from the 1965 COLEX (central information reference and control online experiment), first becomes available.

The same set of programs as those used in ORBIT are used to create the ELHILL (named after the Lister Hill National Centre for Biomedical Communications) system, which is used by the National Library of Medicine to launch MEDLARS online, or MEDLINE, and later, by the British Library, for BLAISE (British Library Automated Information Service).

The NLM signs contracts with Western Union and Tymshare to allow regional medical libraries and NLM centres access to the NLM's computers at 300 baud via terminals.

1972

Jon Postel creates the first Telnet specification (RFC 318) entitled: 'Ad hoc Telnet Protocol'. This is developed by the National Centre for Supercomputing Applications (NCSA) to make it easier to log in to remote computers.

The NLM can now support 45 simultaneous users. One hundred institutions use it by the end of 1972.

The Lockheed DIALOG system begins as a commercial online search service, containing databases from the US Office of Education, ERIC (Educational Resources Information Centre), the US National Technical Information Service, NTIS, and the National Agricultural Library, ARICOLA (agricultural online access).

1974

The term 'Internet' is used for the first time.

1976

The CCITT (Consultative Committee for International Telegraphy and Telephony, now the ITU-T, International

Telecommunications Union - Telecommunication Standardization Sector) defines the X.25 protocol for public packet-switched networks.

British TV companies begin Teletext services, originally known as Ceefax for BBC1 and BBC2 and Oracle for ITV.

Prestel, a viewdata service similar in look to Teletext, is also launched around this time by British Telecommunications (BT).

1977

Tymshare starts the Tymnet network.

BLAISE is started to give access to the NLM's MEDLINE database.

1980

The number of online databases reaches 400, offered by 221 database producers, and accessible via 59 search services.

Data-Star is set up by Radio Suisse in Switzerland.

ECHO (the European Commission Host Organization) set up.

1981

Ted Nelson conceptualizes 'Xanadu', a central, pay-per-document hypertext database encompassing all written information.

IBM releases its IBM PC, retailing for $4500. Other personal computers are developed using Unix as their operating system.

The number of online databases reaches 600, offered by 340 database producers, and accessible via 93 search services.

BT sets up PSS (packet switch stream) and IPSS (international packet switching service).

1982

The number of Internet hosts breaks 200.

The first PC LAN (local-area network) is demonstrated at the National Computer Conference by Drew Major, Kyle Powell, and Dale Neibaur. Their software eventually becomes Novell's Netware.

Domain Name Service (DNS) is outlined in RFC 830 after being developed at the University of Wisconsin.

The number of online databases reaches 1350, offered by 718 database producers, and accessible via 213 search services.

BT launches their Telecom Gold email service.

1983

The number of Internet hosts breaks 300.

The Internet becomes a reality when ARPANET (Advanced Research Projects Agency network) is split into military and civilian sections. Previously, all Internet hosts had been military.

Berkeley releases Unix 4.2BSD, including TCP/IP (transmission control protocol/Internet protocol).

1984

The number of Internet hosts breaks 1000.

William Gibson coins the term Cyberspace in the novel Neuromancer.

The number of online databases reaches 1878, offered by 927 database producers, and accessible via 272 search services.

JANET (the Joint Academic Network) is created in April, using the X.25 protocol, and provides access, initially at 9.6 Kbps, to about 50 university and polytechnic sites.

1985

Databases on CD-ROM are first made available.

The number of online databases reaches 2453, offered by 1189 database producers, and accessible via 362 search services.

1986

The number of Internet hosts breaks 5000.

The number of online databases reaches 2901, offered by 1379 database producers, and accessible via 454 search services.

1987

The number of Internet hosts breaks 10,000.

The number of online databases reaches 3369, offered by 1568 database producers, and accessible via 528 search services.

FT Information Online acquires Datasolve Information Online and offers its FT Profile service providing full-text online coverage of some of the major newspapers in the UK and USA.

Start of the ADONIS (article delivery over network information systems) project by the British Library, which aims to supply 200 medical journals on weekly CD-ROMs.

1988

The first transatlantic fibre optic cable linking North America and Europe is completed. It can handle 40,000 telephone calls simultaneously.

The number of online databases reaches 3893, offered by 1723 database producers, and accessible via 576 search services.

Knight-Ridder acquires DIALOG Information Services Inc.

1989

The number of Internet hosts breaks 100,000.

The first gateways between private electronic mail carriers and the Internet are established.

The first web project proposal is distributed by Tim Berners-Lee at CERN (European Oranization for Nuclear Research).

The Joint Network Team (for JANET) proposes creation of SuperJANET, a high-performance wide-area network based on optical fibres.

1990

Archie, a program that locates files at anonymous FTP sites by filename (or string expression) search, is released by Peter Deutsch, Alan Emtage, and Bill Heelan.

The first world wide web software is created by Tim Berners-Lee.

1991

The number of Internet hosts breaks 600,000.

Wide area information servers (WAIS) are invented by Brewster Kahle.

Gopher, a way of presenting files as a hierarchically structured list over the Internet, is released by Paul Lindner and Mark P. McCahill from the University of Minnesota.

JANET IP Service (JIPS) is introduced.

1992

The number of Internet hosts break 1,000,000.

Veronica (very easy rodent-orientated net-wide index to computerized archives), a gopher space search tool, is released by the University of Nevada.

The term 'surfing the Net' is coined by Jean Armour Polly.

Implementation of SuperJANET using BT. Speeds initially start at 34Mbps using a data network and an ATM (asynchronous transfer mode) one. Will expand to 155Mbps in a few years.

1993

The number of Internet hosts break 2,000,000.

There are about 50 http (hypertext transfer protocol) servers.

Web traffic measures 0.1% of NSF (National Science Foundation) backbone traffic.

The world wide web is presented at Online Publishing '93 in Pittsburgh.

InterNIC is created to register domain names, beginning at a rate of almost 400 per month.

Mosaic is released for Macintosh and Windows.

There are now over 500 known http servers.

1994

The web grows at a 342,634% annual growth. Gopher grows at 997%.

Marc Andressen and Jim Clark form Mosaic Communications Corp (now Netscape).

The number of Internet hosts breaks 3,000,000.

Domain names are being registered at the rate of 2000 per month.

1995

The number of Internet hosts breaks 4,000,000.

Http (web) packets pass FTP (file transfer protocol) traffic to be the largest Internet protocol.

1996

The number of Internet hosts breaks 9,000,000.

1997

The number of Internet hosts breaks 16,000,000.

Major sources used

Adams, R (1990) Communication and delivery systems for librarians, Gower, ISBN 0-566-05750-6.

Somewhat out of date, but there is a very useful historical section in Chapter 1, entitled 'The development of communications technology'. The rest of the book is worth a quick read.

Anderberg, A (1999) History of the Internet and Web (found at: **http://www.geocities.com/~anderberg/ant/history**).

Well worth looking at. The author is constantly updating this page which has useful links to other books and references, as well as links to other useful web pages.

Hartley, R J, et all (1990) Online searching: principles and practice, Bowker-Saur, ISBN 0-408-02290-6.

Mostly out of date now, but contains a very useful Chapter 2, entitled 'History and development of the online industry'. The other chapters in the book are also worth perusing, as the basic principles remain the same.

Appendix 2
Modems

Introduction

This appendix concentrates on how modems work. This guide to modems is necessarily brief, but covers all the main points.

Even though many online searchers may well be connected directly to the Internet at their workplace, a great deal of searching is also carried out by librarians in organizations that are not connected to the Internet, or the world, except by modems. Modems are also, almost always, used at home to connect to the Internet.

They can be used to connect any type of personal computer (PC), including desk-top PCs, laptops, Apple Macintoshes, Amigas and so on. It is, therefore, useful to know how a modem works.

What is a modem?

The word modem derives from *modulator demodulator*, which refers to the alteration (modulation) of the signals that are sent between your PC and other PCs or large mainframe-type hosts.

The modem is a device used to convert the digital signals from your PC into analogue signals that are then transmitted via ordinary phone lines. At the other end, another modem converts these analogue signals back into digital signals that the receiving PC, or host computer, can read.

How do modems connect with each other?

In order for modems to talk to each other, standards are required. Modem standards are set by the ITU-T (International Telecommunications Union - Telecommunication Standardization Sector) committee, formerly know as the CCITT (Consultative Committee for International Telegraphy and Telephony) committee.

These standards usually set the speed of connection, how error correction and data compression are handled, and what command sets are used to control the modems. These terms are detailed below.

Speed of connection

This is always an important feature to bear in mind when buying a modem. A modem's speed is measured in bits per second (bps). The faster the speed, the quicker the transmission and the lower the costs. (Less time spent online or more data received and transmitted in the same time.)

As mentioned above, the ITU-T sets internationally recognized standards for modem communication — their 'V' series. These are listed in Table A2.

Table A2 *Modem speeds*

ITU-T standard	Speed
V.21	300 bps
V.22	1200 bps
V.22 bis	2400 bps
V.23	1200/75 bps
V.32	9.6 Kbps
V.32 bis	14.4 Kbps
V.32 terbo	19.2 Kbps
V.34	28.8 Kbps
V.34 + (enhanced)	33.6 Kbps
V.90	56 Kbps

Nowadays modems of 28.8 Kbps or higher are common with most of the new modems being sold running at 56 Kbps.

As an aside, when dealing with computers and storage, we tend to talk mainly in terms of bytes and not bits. Perhaps a truer measure of speed would be how many bytes per second a modem can transmit and/or receive.

- A bit (abbreviation 'b') is either of the two digits, 0 and 1, in the binary number system. The bit, or binary digit, is the smallest unit of storage in any binary system within a computer.

- A byte (abbreviation 'B') is usually defined as a character, ie a single letter, number, or other symbol, and is usually 8 bits long.

From the above, therefore, a speed of 33.6 Kbps (33,600 bits per second) would be equivalent to a speed of 33,600 divided by 8, bytes (characters) per second — 4200 bytes per second (4.2 KBps). Therefore, a file of 840 KB should take about 200 seconds, or 3 minutes and 20 seconds, to be transmitted.

However, factors such as noise on the line can adversely affect transmission, causing modems to communicate at slower speeds then those for which they are rated.

Communication is usually at the highest mutual speed possible. The deciding factor is usually which of the two modems has the slowest speed. The modems will negotiate this when starting their communication. We hear this as a high-pitched whistle that changes to crackles and then stops when communication is established.

When setting the speed of your modem, in the communications software that you will be using, it is almost always advisable to set the speed higher than that at which your modem will connect. This helps when the modems start negotiating and you will usually find that your modem will then connect at its advertised speed.

Error correction

The quality of telecommunication lines varies quite considerably, and some means of handling errors, caused by noise and other factors, needed to be developed.

Error correction is used to check data as it is received, to make sure that it is correct. There are two standards in use today, one is the ITU-T's V.42 error correction, the other is known as MNP4.

Both are generally compatible, and modems using the different methods usually work properly.

Error correction will, of course, slow up your speed of transmission, possible by as much as half, since the receiving modem needs to signal the sending modem that it has received everything correctly.

Data compression

One way to get around the loss of speed due to error correction is to use data compression. This, as the name suggests, compresses data so that more data can be sent at a given speed. Once again there are two standards, but this time they are incompatible: an ITU-T standard called V.42 bis and another widely used standard called MNP5.

As an example, using V.42 bis data compression on a V.32 (9.6 Kbps) modem will raise the theoretical throughput of the modem to 14.4 Kbps.

As with all of the above, data compression can only be used at the highest mutual speed.

Command sets

Command sets are codes that allow your communication software to control the modem. The AT command set is the most widely used; it was invented by Hayes.

However, some modem manufacturers have implemented the AT command sets on their modems in different ways to cope with increased speed, etc. The Hayes AT command set, however, still remains as the industry standard. If in doubt, consult your modems manual.

Flow control

Most modems communicate asynchronously. This means that they talk to each other one at a time. The flow of communication can start and stop and include varying intervals of silence without causing communication problems.

Modems are usually used to transfer files or streams of data from one place to another. These streams can be very large and fast, and this can cause the receive buffer in the modem to clog up. This will result in data being lost, simply because the modem is not receiving what is being sent — it is trying to digest what it has already received.

What stops data being lost if too much is sent at once? The way around this is to use some form of 'flow' control, whereby signals are sent telling the sending modem that the receiving modem's buffer is full and to wait until receipt of a signal telling it to start again.

There have been various ways to describe this flow control, but there are two main types: software flow control and hardware flow control.

Software flow control

Mainly used with modem speeds of 2400 bps or less, this is also known as Xon/Xoff. This is set using the AT command set or via the communications software used.

Do not use this type of flow control with modems running at 9.6 Kbps or faster. They should use hardware flow control.

Hardware flow control

This is nearly always used by modern modems. It is also known as RTS/CTS (ready to send/clear to send). Again this can be set via the AT commands or via the communications software used.

Do not use this type of flow control with modems running at 2400 bps or less.

What other communication parameters are required?

There are three other communication parameters that are important in modem-to-modem communications. These are: the number of data bits, the number of stop bits, and the type of parity checking used.

Number of data bits

Computers use binary digits (bits) to communicate with their peripheral devices, modems included. A complete character would consist of a series of '0' and '1' data bits arranged in a specific pattern. The capital letter A is defined by the bit pattern 10000001.

Normally modems have to agree on how many data bits comprise a character. In asynchronous communications this tends to be 8 data bits.

Number of stop bits

Asynchronous communication uses stop bits and start bits to indicate the beginning and end of each transmitted character. This adds another 2 bits to each character, making 10 bits needed to be sent to get one character down the line.

Therefore, the discussion of bits and bytes on p. 127-8, whilst correct, doesn't tell the whole story. If 10 bits are required for each character, a speed of 33.6 Kbps would then equate to 3.36 KBps.

Parity checking

Parity checking is a system that was used to ensure that the character received was the actual character sent. The parity checking bit was added to each character's set of data bits and would be processed at the other end to see if anything had been changed.

Use of parity checking has mainly been superceded by error-correction protocols. However, instructions for accessing an online service will still talk about which parity should be used, eg no parity, even parity, odd parity, space parity, and so on.

To save bother, always assume that the parity will be 'no parity' (sometimes known as 'none'), unless told otherwise.

All of this boils down quite simply to something very easy to remember: 8-N-1. That means 8 data bits, no parity, and 1 stop bit.

Internal or external modems

Modems are made in mainly two distinct types: internal modems and external modems (the PCMCIA modem is more of a hybrid).

Internal modems

Internal modems are PC cards that can be installed into spare expansion slots in the backs of most PCs. Some laptop computers have built-in modems, but these usually can't be accessed by the user.

Usually, jumper switches must be set to select the appropriate com port and interrupt setting. The com port is the channel by which data is accepted into the central processing unit of the PC, and the interrupt setting is the means by which the modem tells the computer that it has data it needs to deliver.

Computers have four com ports, ie COM1, COM2, COM3, and COM4. However, there are only two hardware interrupts to service these ports: namely IRQ3 and IRQ4. Usually COM1 and COM3 are controlled by IRQ4 and COM2 and COM4 by IRQ3.

Only two com ports can be used at any one time. Usually the internal modem is set to IRQ3 and COM4 to avoid conflict with anything that may be using COM1, eg a printer or mouse. This does mean, however, that COM2 will not work when your modem is running.

To install the modem card, you need to first set the appropriate jumpers in order to select which com port and interrupt setting you intend to use. Then remove the cover of your PC and install the card into one of the free expansion slots. Usually one of the connectors on the back panel of the card is used to connect the modem to your telephone line.

You may also need to set some DIP switches, which may, or may not, appear on the card back panel. They look like miniature light switches reduced to about 1 or 2 mm in size. These can be quite complicated and you may need help with them.

Other types of modem are switchless and rely upon using the AT command set to issue commands to set up the modem via communications software. However, in the event of power surges, these modems may lose their configuration and may need to be configured from scratch.

Advantages

You don't need a separate power supply for an internal modem card — it is powered by the PC.

You don't require a cable to connect the modem to the PC. It is already connected.

Disadvantages

There are usually no indicator lights on internal modems to show you if you have a connection and whether anything is being sent or received.

You have to remove your computer cover to install the modem and setting the modem to the correct com port and IRQ can be very tricky, especially if there are conflicts with other cards.

If the modem appears to be faulty it's not very easy just to replace it and see if another modem works. You have to open the computer cover and remove it.

External modems

Most PCs nowadays come with one or two serial ports situated on the back of the computer. They are usually labelled COM1 and COM2, respectively (although not always). They will also be of the 9 pin D socket variety and not the old 25 pin D socket.

They will usually be supplied with the correct modem cable — usually a 25 pin male connector at the modem end and a 9 pin female connector at the PC end.

If there are two serial ports, choose the one labelled COM2. If not, simply connect the modem to the serial port. You will also need to attach the power cable and also the telephone line.

You are now ready to use the modem.

Advantages

You don't need to remove the PC's cover for installation.

Most external modems have a good display which shows the connection process and whether or not the modem is actually sending and receiving data.

If you think your modem has developed a fault, you can easily swop one modem for another. Usually the cables will fit any modem.

Disadvantages

You will need a separate power supply for your modem.

You will end up with even more cables which can look very messy.

PCMCIA modems

PCMCIA (Personal Computer Memory Card International Association) cards are roughly credit card in size and shape, and come in varying thicknesses.

Most modern laptop computers will have either two type I or 1 type II PCMCIA slots. Into these slots you can put PCMCIA cards containing extra memory, hard disks, modems, etc.

The beauty of this type of modem is its size — no bigger than a credit card. It can be permanently left in the PCMCIA slot, and usually connects to the phone line via a very small connector. It can also be linked to GSM (global system for mobile communications) phones for complete mobile communications.

PCMCIA modems come in all speeds and all types, so using one won't put you at a disadvantage. However, connecting the modem to a phone line can be awkward.

Appendix 3
Books and journals on online/Internet searching

Introduction

This appendix simply lists books, reports, and journals on the topic of online searching and searching the Internet. This list should not be seen as exhaustive, as only books published in the UK have been referenced and we have been very selective about the journals.

For the books and reports, the information provided consists of author(s), date of publication, title of item, edition, publisher, and ISBN. Items are listed by date of publication, so that the most recent publications are at the top of each list.

We have listed items back to 1990 for books on online searching because the basic principles of how to search remain the same. However, we have only listed books published in the last two years for items on searching the Internet, because the Internet is such a fast-moving field that any item over two years old is liable to be already out of date.

For journals, the information provided consists of title of journal, publisher, address, telephone number and fax (where given), email contact, and website address, plus a bit of blurb about the journal. Items are listed by name of journal.

Books on online searching

Chowdhury, G G (1999) *Introduction to modern information retrieval*, Library Association Publishing, ISBN 1856043185.

Houghton, J M and Houghton, R S (1999) *Decision points: Boolean logic for computer users and beginning online searching*, Eurospan, ISBN 1563086727.

Miller, M (1999) *The complete idiot's guide to online search secrets*, Prentice Hall, ISBN 0789720426.

Walker, G and Janes, J (1999) *Online retrieval: a dialogue of theory and practice*, Eurospan, ISBN 1563086573.

Armstrong, C J and Hartley, R J (1997) *Keyguide to information sources in online and CD-ROM database searching*, 2nd edn, Mansell, ISBN 0720122074.

Ridley, D D (1996) *Online searching: a scientist's perspective: a guide for the chemical and life sciences*, Wiley, ISBN 0471965200.

Dyer, H and Bouchet, M-L (1995) *A comparison between the perceived value of information retrieved via end-user searching of CD-ROMs and mediated online searching*, British Library, Research and Development Department, British Library R&D Report: 6208.

Lescher, J F (1995) *Online market research: cost-effective searching of the Internet and online databases*, Addison-Wesley, ISBN 0201489295.

Armstrong, C J and Large, J A (eds) (1992) *Manual of online search strategies*, 2nd edn, Ashgate, ISBN 1857420071.

Chamis, A Y (1991) *Vocabulary control and search strategies in online searching*, Greenwood, ISBN 0313254907.

Orton, D (1991) *Online searching in science and technology: an introductory guide to equipment, databases, and search techniques*, British Library, ISBN 0712308024.

Hartley, R J et al (1990) *Online searching: principles and practice*, Bowker-Saur, ISBN 0408022906.

Books on searching the Internet

Ackermann, E and Hartman, K (1999) *The information specialist's guide to searching and researching on the Internet and the World Wide Web*, Fitzroy Dearborn.

Bradley, P (1999) *The advanced Internet searcher's handbook*, Library Association Publishing, ISBN 1856043029.

Burke, J (1999) *Intronet: a beginner's guide to searching the Internet*, Neal-Schuman Publishers, ISBN 1555703518.

Cooke, A (1999) *A guide to finding quality information on the Internet: selection and evaluation strategies*, Library Association Publishing, ISBN 1856042677.

Hill, B (1999) *Internet searching for dummies*, Transworld, ISBN 0764504789.

Sharpe, C C (1999) *Patent, trademark and copyright searching on the Internet*, McFarland, ISBN 0786407573.

Blakeman, K (1998) *Search strategies for the Internet: how to identify essential resources more effectively*, RBA Information Services, ISBN 0952719126.

McBride, P K (1998) *Searching the Internet made simple*, Made Simple, ISBN 0750637943.

Salehi, J (1998) *Searching the Internet: an in-depth guide for professionals, scientists and researchers*, AP Professional, ISBN 0126154600.

Journals on online/Internet searching

EContent, Online, Inc., 462 Danbury Rd., Wilton, CT 06897-4007; tel: +1 203 761 1466, +1 800 248 8466; fax: +1 203 761 1444; e-mail: dbmag@onlineinc.com; URL: **http://www.ecmag.net**.

EContent (formerly Database) magazine is written for 'hands on' searchers, managers of information facilities and others who use information technology. It provides practical, how-to advice on effective use of databases and systems, plus innovative tips and techniques, reviews, and product comparison. It covers databases in online, CD-ROM, disk, and tape formats, and resources on the Internet.

The Electronic Library, Learned Information Europe Ltd., Woodside, Hinksey Hill, Oxford OX1 5BE, England; tel: +44 (0)1865 388000; fax: +44 (0)1865 736354; e-mail: subscriptions@learned.co.uk; URL: **http://www.learned.co.uk/tel/index.asp**.

The Electronic Library provides an independent and unbiased assessment of today's automated library and information centre, and contains informative reviews to help you make your choice when investing in new technology for your library.

Articles by skilled industry experts and users cover all aspects of computerization and networking in libraries, including the growing field of optical media. Practical advice, actual user experience, useful information and specific application recommendations supplement research papers, which are peer-reviewed. *The Electronic Library* provides news and reviews to keep you up to date with new products, trends, and services.

EMedia Professional, Online, Inc., 213 Danbury Rd., Wilton, CT 06897-4007; tel: +1 203 761 1466; fax: +1 203 761 1444; e-mail: emedia@onlineinc.com; URL: **http://www.emediapro.ne**t.

EMedia Professional covers the tools and technologies that professionals use to publish, archive, distribute, and network digital content. The magazine is for producers and the business users of CD-ROM, CD-Recordable, DVD, CD-ROM/online hybrid, and Internet-based electronic media applications and products. *EMedia Professional* offers meaningful analyses, unique case studies, critical reviews, and comprehensive new products and emerging technology reporting.

Fulltext Sources Online, Information Today, Inc., 143 Marlton Pike, Medford, NJ 08055-8750; tel: +1 609 654 6266; fax: +1 609 654 4309; e-mail: custservl@infotoday.com; URL: **http://www.infotoday.com**.

Fulltext Sources Online is published each January and July with a complete new edition. It lists over 11,600 newspapers, journals, magazines, newsletters, and newswires found online in full-text. The directory covers the following aggregators and content providers: Burrelle's Broadcast Database, Data-Star, DIALOG, Dow Jones Interactive, EDD, FT Profile, Gale, GBI, Genios, Infomart Online, Lexis-Nexis, Nikkei Net Interactive, OCLC, Ovid, Profound, QL Systems, Questel, Reuters Business Briefing, STN International, and Westlaw. It also tracks journals that have free Internet archives.

Information World Review, Learned Information Europe Ltd., Woodside, Hinksey Hill, Oxford OX1 5BE, England; tel: +44 (0)1865 388000; fax: +44 (0)1865 736354; e-mail: custserv@infotoday.com; URL: **http://www.iwr.co.uk/iwr/**.

Reports on the information industry events and trends, software companies, electronic and optical publishing, new products, databases, networks, telecommunications developments and library automation.

Online, Online, Inc., 462 Danbury Rd., Wilton, CT 06897; tel: +1 203 761 1466, +1 800 248 8466; fax: +1 203 761 1444; e-mail: info@onlineinc.com;

URL: **http://www.onlineinc.com/onlinemag/index.html**.

Online is written for information professionals and provides articles, product reviews, case studies, evaluation, and informed opinion about selecting, using, and managing electronic information products, plus industry and professional information about online database systems, CD-ROMs, and the Internet.

Online & CD-ROM Review, Learned Information Europe Ltd., Woodside, Hinksey Hill, Oxford OX1 5BE, England; tel: +44 (0)1865 388100; fax: +44 (0)1865 736354; e-mail: subscriptions@learned.co.uk;
URL: **http://www.learned.co.uk/olr/index.asp**.

Online & CD-ROM Review covers the use and management of online and optical information retrieval systems, the training and education of online users, the development of search aids, the creation and marketing of databases, the policy affecting continued development of systems and networks, and the development of new standards for the profession.

Searcher, Information Today, Inc., 143 Old Marlton Pike, Medford, NJ 08055; tel: +1 609 654 6266; fax: +1 609 654 4309; e-mail: quint@netcom.com; custserv@infotoday.com; URL: **http://www.infotoday.com/searcher/srchrtop.htm**.

Searcher is a unique publication that explores and deliberates on a comprehensive range of issues important to the professional database-searcher. The magazine is targeted at experienced, knowledgeable searchers, and combines evaluations of data content with discussions of delivery media. Searcher includes evaluated online news, searching tips and techniques, reviews of search-aid software and database documentation, revealing interviews with leaders and entrepreneurs of the industry, and trenchant editorials. Whatever the experienced database searcher needs to know to get the job done is covered in Searcher.

Appendix 4
Major online database host services

Introduction

This appendix lists 17 major online hosts and their contact details. We have listed their UK office, where possible. If the address is for an office outside the UK, then the country is also given.

The arrangement is purely alphabetical and lists the hosts' name, address, telephone and fax numbers and their website address.

Major online host services

BIDS
BUCS Building
University of Bath
Bath
BA2 7AY
Tel: +44 (0)1225 826267
Fax: +44 (0)1225 826283
URL: **http://www.bids.ac.uk**

Blaise
The British Library
Boston Spa
Wetherby
West Yorkshire
LS23 7BQ
Tel: +44 (0)1937 546585
Fax: +44 (0)1937 546586
URL: **http://blaiseweb.bl.uk**

Cambridge Scientific Abstracts (CSA)
40 London Road
Newbury
Berkshire
RG14 1LA
Tel: +44 (0)1635 262711
Fax: +44 (0)1635 262717
URL: **http://www.csa.com**

Derwent Customer Services
Derwent Information
14 Great Queen Street
London
WC2B 5DF
Tel: +44 (0)20 7424 2347
Fax: +44 (0)20 7344 2972
URL: **http://www.derwent.com**

The DIALOG Corporation & Data-Star Headquarters
The Communications Building
48 Leicester Square
London
WC2H 7DB
Tel: +44 (0)20 7930 690
Fax: +44 (0)20 7930 6006
URL: **http://www.dialog.com**

DIMDI
Weißhausstr. 27
D-50939 Köln
Germany
Tel: +49 (0) 221 47241
Fax: +49 (0) 221 411429
URL: **http://www.dimdi.de**

EBSCO Online
General Manager
4th Floor
Kingmaker House
Station Road
New Barnet
EN5 1NZ
Tel: +44 (0)20 8447 4200
Fax: +44 (0)20 8440 2205
URL: **http://www.ebsco.com**

EINS (European Information Network Services)
DIALTECH
The British Library
St. Pancras
96 Euston Road
London
NW1 2DB
Tel: +44 (0)20 7412 7946 or 412 7951
Fax: +44 (0)20 7412 7947
URL: **http://www.eins.org**

Financial Times Information
Fitzroy House
13-17 Epworth Street
London
EC2A 4DL
Tel: +44 (0)20 7825 8000
URL: **http://www.info.ft.com**

ISI (Institute for Scientific Information)
ISI Europe
Brunel Science Park
Uxbridge
UB8 3PQ
Tel: +44 (0)1895 270016
Fax: +44 (0)1895 256710
URL: **http://www.isinet.com**

LEXIS-NEXIS
PO Box 933
Dayton
OH 45401-0933
USA
Tel: +1 937 865 6800
Fax: +1 800 227 9597
URL: **http://www.lexis-nexis.com**

National Library of Medicine
8600 Rockville Pike
Bethesda
MD 20894
USA
Tel: +1 888 346 3656
Fax: +1 301 594 5983
URL: **http://www.nlm.nih.gov**

OCLC Europe, the Middle East & Africa
7th Floor
Tricorn House
51-53 Hagley Road
Birmingham
B16 8TP
Tel: +44 (0)121 456 4656
Fax: +44 (0)121 456 4680
URL: **http://www.oclc.org**

OVID Technologies United Kingdom and Ireland

Ovid Technologies Ltd
107 Hammersmith Grove
London
W6 ONQ
Tel: +44 (0)20 8748-3777
Fax: +44 (0)20 8748-2302
URL: **http://www.ovid.com**

Questel-Orbit

MineSoft Ltd
Worple Court
South Worple Way
London
SW14 8NG
Tel: +44 (0)20 8404 0651
Fax: +44 (0)20 8404 0681
URL: **http://www.questel.orbit.com**

SilverPlatter Information

Merlin House
20 Belmont Terrace
Chiswick
London W4 4PH
Tel: +44 (0)208 585 6400
Fax: +44 (0)208 585 6640
URL: **http://www.silverplatter.com**

STN International FIZ Karlsruhe

Fachinformationszentrum (FIZ) Karlsruhe Gesellschaft für
    wissenschaftlich-technische Information mbH
PO Box 2465
76012 Karlsruhe
Germany
Tel.: +49 (0)72 478080
Fax: +49 (0)72 47808259
URL: **http://www.fiz-karlsruhe.de**

Index

A Guide to Finding Quality Information on the Internet

Alison Cooke

'Cooke has produced a valuable work which should not only be essential reading for any student of information science, but which also gives plentiful advice for those undertaking literature searches or using the Internet as an information source.'

Internet Resources Newsletter

This easy-to-use Internet guide will not only show you how to access the net and find information, but also how to sort the quality sites from the mass of junk available. Uniquely, the book suggests a system of criteria developed through empirical research and summarized in useful checklists, for selecting and evaluating a wide range of information resources. It looks at the advantages and disadvantages of search facilities such as search engines, subject catalogues and directories, rating and reviewing services, subject-based gateway services and virtual libraries, and it covers:

- issues and problems of information quality
- using a range of search facilities to maximize quality information retrieval
- assessing the quality of an information source
- evaluating particular types of sources.

Alison Cooke is currently an information skills trainer in the Medical Library at the Royal Free Hospital and Royal Free University College of Medicine in London. She has recently completed a PhD looking at quality issues associated with information available via the Internet at the Department of Information and Library Studies, University of Wales Aberystwyth.

1999; 176pp; paperback; ISBN 1-85604-267-7; £29.95

The Advanced Internet Searcher's Handbook

Phil Bradley

'*An invaluable guide to searching on the Net – a must for all Net researchers*'
Internet.Works
'*What an excellent text this is!* The Advanced Internet Searcher's Handbook *contains a great deal of useful information, facts and tips.*'
Internet Resources Newsletter

Despite all the hype about how easy the Internet is to use, and how you can find almost anything you want, unless you are a skilled searcher, this is far from the case.

This handbook teaches you how to search the Internet more effectively by giving you a better understanding of how search engines and related software work, allowing you to use them to improve your search techniques.

The text is packed with helpful visual devices such as screenshots, step-by-step examples, side bars, icons and search tips, and every opportunity is taken to indicate useful websites and valuable utilities.

Topics covered include:

- the main search engines
- other available databases on the Internet
- intelligent agents
- virtual libraries and gateways
- how to get the best out of popular browsers
- USENET newsgroups and mailing lists
- future developments of the Internet.

To be read from cover to cover or dipped into when needed, this guide will be of use to all those searching the Internet for information, whether you are taking your first steps or are becoming more expert. Although the text pays particular atttention to the use information professionals can make of the Internet, it will be helpful to anyone who wishes to find information quickly.

Phil Bradley has a background as an information professional and has worked in the field of electronic publishing for the last ten years. He is currently an independent Internet consultant and is well known throughout the industry for his talks, training courses, lectures, books and articles on various aspects of electronic publishing and the Internet.

1999; 248pp; paperback; 1-85604-302-9; £29.95